THE TINKERTOY COMPUTER

AND OTHER MACHINATIONS

THE TINKERTOY COMPUTER
AND OTHER MACHINATIONS

A. K. DEWDNEY

W. H. FREEMAN AND COMPANY
NEW YORK

Library of Congress Cataloging-in-Publication Data

Dewdney, A. K.
    The Tinkertoy computer and other machinations.
    [A.K. Dewdney].
        p. cm.
    Includes index.
    ISBN 0-7167-2489-8. — ISBN 0-7167-2491-X (pbk.)
    1. Computers. I. Scientific American. II. Algorithm.
    III. Title.
    QA76.5.D458 1993
    004—dc20   93-10478
                                                            CIP

Printed in the United States of America

1 2 3 4 5 6 7 8 9 0 VB 9 9 8 7 6 5 4 3

004
D515ti

258177

CONTENTS

THE TINKERTOY COMPUTER

AND OTHER MACHINATIONS

THE HIDDEN AGENDA

The term "machinations" in this book's title refers first to the marvellous machines called computers—in all their manifestations. The term refers secondly to my own machinations. Until this third book of computer recreations, I have kept my agenda hidden.

During my career as a computer scientist, I have tried, as many academics do, to express difficult concepts in simple and engaging examples with a recreational flavor. Balanced with more (rather than less) pedestrian material, this approach has, I hope, helped to make computer science a bit more fun and interesting for the few thousand students I have taught over the years.

In 1984, when I was invited to write the Computer Recreations column for *Scientific American* magazine, the recreational approach seemed perfect—it already matched that side of my lecturing style. Moreover, I saw it as a golden opportunity to bring computer science to a new set of "students," a worldwide readership that numbered in the millions. But here the emphasis was reversed. It was recreation first and education second—and a very distant second if the columns threatened to become miniature lectures. I was forced to go underground. Every recreation, from Tinkertoy computers to programmed cartoons, became a secret vehicle for teaching anything from computer logic to graphic programming methods. That was my hidden agenda.

Later, when *Scientific American* changed the name of the column to Mathematical Recreations, I followed the same secret course, hiding proof techniques in the alleys of Golygon City and concealing research methods in the innards of two-dimensional cats.

In both columns the machinations paid off. Readers seemed to enjoy themselves, even if they didn't always realize the full importance of what they had just learned. The trouble lay in the word "recreations." It put readers at a serious contextual disadvantage. If my regular students knew that, despite my recreational ways, lectures in computer science were serious stuff, too many of my new students may have been overly influenced by that word, especially when it came to the heavier, philosophical ideas. How seriously would you treat anything Descartes said at a party? "Here's a good one: I think therefore I am. Ha ha."

I have always been attracted by certain philosophical themes that arise from computing and mathematics. In this latest collection of columns, I have decided to come clean about four of the themes, to stop treating them as schemes. Here they are, boldly stated and briefly described.

MATTER COMPUTES: Almost any form of matter may be organized into a computer. You can use tinkertoys, ropes and pulleys, even individual molecules. Living things organize their own matter, not only into muscle fibers and bone marrow, but into brains. In the most general sense, at least, brains compute. From a purely computational point of view, evolution may turn out to be nothing less than the emergence of mind from matter. With a surprisingly small investment in computation, matter may be made to behave with something like intelligence.

MATTER MISBEHAVES: We can simulate a great many physical and dynamical systems by computer, even a game of golf or a starship combat. Viewed as predictive models, however, computer programs have one major limitation. We have only recently discovered that some dynamical systems are capable of chaos. This form of dynamical misbehavior amounts to a veil that hides a system's future from our view forever. Even if we cannot look behind it, we can see the veil itself. It has fractal embroidery.

MATHEMATICS MATTERS: Explicitly or implicitly, mathematics informs every worthwhile scientific idea. Besides being an amazing subject in itself, mathematics determines what is science and what is not. Computer science, which some view as a branch of mathematics, derives its major conceptual machinery from mathematics. Luckily, even adventures in pure thought may be disguised as recreations, from the spheres of Dandelin to the flexagons of Connelly.

COMPUTERS CREATE: From a sociological point of view, we are not surprised to find that some people program computers to play discrete music, paint pixellated pictures, or to converse in patchwork speech sewn from human fragments. Whether the music springs from chaos, the faces from files or the speech from random numbers, there is a dilemma: Are computers invading the arts or are the arts invading computers? You can have it both ways, but be warned! The future holds sights, sounds, and stories more bizarre than we can imagine. And the creative act will not always be human.

Of the 23 chapters comprising the present collection, 18 originally appeared as articles in *Scientific American* and five appeared in *Algorithm*, the recreational programming magazine. The chapters have been organized into themes and each throws a light on its theme, illuminating it from a special angle.

Most of the chapters contain recipes or algorithms from which readers can construct programs. One of the chapters (A Game of Micro-Miniature Golf) contains a working program so that beginners in the art of programming may understand how to convert an algorithm into a program in the language of their choice.

Neither the author nor the publisher will assume responsibility for career-change decisions inspired by reading this book.

MATTER COMPUTES

To say that matter computes means, in part, that we get it to compute by constructing the bits and pieces of matter that make up a computer. But it also means that nature itself seems able to do the same thing, insofar as brains amount to computers. If we ever succeed in constructing what critics would cheerfully admit to be a brain, we will have recapitulated our own evolution. Mind will have crept into matter by a new route.

The first two chapters hint at the astonishing variety of means by which computers may be constructed. We may build computers not only from silicon circuits but from Tinkertoy kits and even from systems of ropes and pulleys. In a subject called computer logic we learn that from a few simple logical gates such as AND, OR, and NOT we may construct combinational circuits to perform arithmetic and memory functions. We may even build the central processing unit whose chief task is to run programs. There are basic combinational circuits in rods and spools, also in ropes and pulleys.

The next chapter, on minds, machines, and metaphysics, forms a bridge between the animate and the inanimate. In it, readers discover another computer made out of an extremely odd billiard table. The billiard ball computer bolsters the argument of a prominent theoretical physicist that human brains cannot be computers. The objections are met here with a determined resistance from the artificial intelligence community. In the process of debate, readers learn valuable criteria for deciding when we have met the goal.

Whatever the status of human brains, the insectoids have already arrived. Metallic insects with brains of silicon do not exactly refute the critics of artificial intelligence, even if they (the insectoids) *act* like insects. But they show how behavior can be orchestrated from the interaction of microchips, motors, and metal legs. The latest progress in robotics springs from two new evolutionary constraints of our own: Keep it simple and keep it cheap!

By what machination might we turn a computer into a brain? Should we be surprised if neural nets turn out to be the scheme of choice? The next chapter in this suite takes the gloves off and shows how to construct a network of some forty neurons that learns how to convert between coordinate systems — a humble but not unimpressive task. In spite of certain drawbacks to the neural net paradigm, some manufacturers have begun to construct neural chips.

Because real environments impose such tremendous computational demands on intelligent machines, we are still a long way from putting more advanced brains (neural net or not) into insectoids. We turn, therefore, to wholly abstract creatures that contend with a much simpler environment, an infinite checkerboard. Tur-mites embody the potential for full computational power over this simple terrain. Singly or in pairs, their built-in Turing machines drive them to paint the screen red and to build the most intricate mounds imaginable.

Some chapters suggest extra reading for those who would like to pursue the nuts and bolts of specific methods or to probe the key debate of the twenty-first century.

1

THE TINKERTOY COMPUTER

I first had that experience (universality of computation)
before I went to school. There weren't any
(computers) yet, but we had toy construction sets.
One was called TinkerToy. . . . What's strange is that
those spools and sticks are enough to make anything.

MARVIN MINSKY, in preface to *LogoWorks*

How many of us remember Tinkertoys, those down-home kits of colored wooden sticks and spools with holes in them? Amid our childhood constructions of towers or cranes, how many of us pondered the outer limits of the Tinkertoy world? Did we conceive of contraptions that reached the ceiling? Perhaps, but we lacked the kits or the time to make it happen. Such a Tinkertoy fantasy took place in 1980 when a student group from the Massachusetts Institute of Technology constructed a computer entirely (well, almost entirely) out of Tinkertoys!

From a distance the Tinkertoy computer resembles a childhood fantasy gone wild or, as one of the group members remarked, a spool-and-stick version of the "space slab" from the movie *2001: A Space Odyssey*. Unlike the alien monolith, the computer plays a mean game of tic-tac-toe. A Tinkertoy framework called the read head clicks and clacks its way down the front of the monolith. At some point the clicking mysteriously stops; a "core piece" within the framework spins and then with a satisfying "kathunk" indirectly kicks an "output duck," a bird-shaped construction. The output duck swings down from its perch so that its beak points at a number — which identifies the computer's next move in a game of tic-tac-toe.

What precisely does the read head scan as it feels its way down the monolith? Nothing less than 48 rows of Tinkertoy "memory spindles" encoding all the critical combinations of X's and O's that might arise during a game (see Figure 1.1). Each spindle is a sequence of smooth spools connected axially by sticks and arranged in nine groups of three each, one group for each square of the tic-tac-toe board. The presence or absence of spools from a group indicates that a corresponding square of the tic-tac-toe board is vacant or is occupied by an X or O.

The Tinkertoy computer is not fully automatic: a human operator must crank the read head up and down and must manage its input. After the computer's opponent makes a move, the operator walks to the front of the machine to adjust the core piece inside the read head, registering the contestant's move. The operator then pulls on a string to cock the core piece for its impending whirl of recognition. When it discovers a memory that matches the current state of the game, the core piece spins, and the computer indicates its move.

The best way to understand how the machine works in detail is to recount the story of its creation at the hands of the M.I.T. students: Erlyne Gee, Edward Hardebeck, Daniel Hillis, Margaret Minsky, and brothers Barry and Brian Silverman. Most of the group has long since graduated and entered various computer professions. Perhaps the best-known team member is Hillis. He was the moving force behind Thinking Machines, Inc., which produces the well-known parallel super-computer called the Connection Machine. (Perhaps Tinkertoys have something to teach us.)

In 1975, when Hillis and Brian Silverman were in their sophomore year, they participated in a class project to build something digital from Tinkertoys. The students sat down to play. One made an inverter—a logic device that converts a binary 1 signal to a 0 signal and conversely. Another made an OR gate; if either of the device's two input signals happened to be a 1, then its output would also be a 1. It quickly became clear to the students that Tinkertoys were "computation universal," the theoretical term for a set of components from which a fully programmable computer can be constructed. Theoretical possibility was one thing, the practical demands of money and time another.

The demands were met in a rather roundabout manner through Hillis's interest in robots. From time to time he had mused openly about building a robot. Word of his idea somehow reached the ear of Harry Loucks, then director of the Mid-America Center in Hot Springs, Ark. Would the students like to construct a robot as a display in the center's museum? The students agreed in principle, but the project seemed too

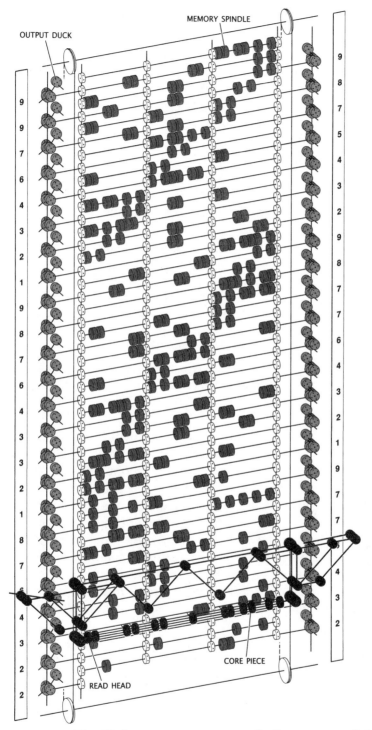

Figure 1.1 The Tinkertoy computer: ready for a game of tic-tac-toe.

complicated. Just then the old Tinkertoy dream resurfaced. Would the center like a computer made out of Tinkertoys instead?

Hillis and company set out to assemble the first Tinkertoy computer in a laboratory at M.I.T. The first model, unlike its successor, was a bulky cube with sides about one meter long. It was impressively complicated. Packed with logic devices made entirely of wooden sticks and spools, the machine signaled its moves by waving nine flags from the top of the framework. The prototype Tinkertoy computer had to be taken apart for the trip to Hot Springs, and once it was reassembled on site, the machine never quite worked properly again. On the other hand, it did make an intriguing exhibit. It has been displayed at the Computer Museum in Boston.

In 1979 Loucks contacted the group again. Could they make a new Tinkertoy computer, one that worked? By this time Silverman was in Ottawa and Hillis in Boston, each pursuing a new career. Over the telephone Hillis and Silverman worked out an improved design. It was to be reliable, and that meant simple. They decided to lay out all the possible tic-tac-toe boards in a row and devise some kind of reading mechanism that would move from row to row until it found a pattern matching the current board. The very act of recognition could trigger a pre-set response.

While Hillis contemplated ways to represent tic-tac-toe boards with digital Tinkertoy components, Silverman analyzed the game. To appreciate the complexities involved even in this childhood pastime, readers might consult the game tree shown in Figure 1.2. In the middle of the tree sits the initial board, a three-by-three grid empty of X's and O's. From this initial board nine new ones can arise, depending on which of the nine squares X plays. The figure shows just three possibilities; the remaining six are rotated versions. Each of the three boards at the second level gives rise to other cases. For example, the board in which X plays the center square and then O plays another square results in two different boards. The remaining two boards at the second level each generate five new boards at the third level.

I pruned many branches from the tic-tac-toe tree by appealing to a symmetry argument: the excluded boards are merely rotations or reflections of the included ones. Symmetry seems simple to humans, but a computer must be programmed or wired to recognize it. In a world of Tinkertoy engineering, symmetry operations would require elaborate structures.

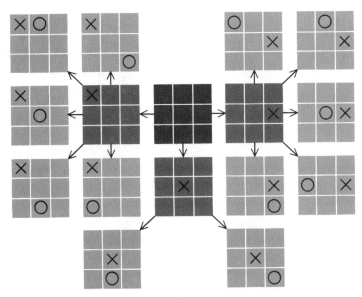

Figure 1.2 First three levels of the tic-tac-toe game tree.

Silverman was dealing with a tree, therefore, that was many times larger than the fragment shown in Figure 1.2. But perseverance paid off, especially when Silverman employed a computer program that analyzed the game of tic-tac-toe and discovered that a great many boards could be collapsed into one by a forced move. Suppose, for example, that two squares in a row contain O's and the third is blank. The contents of the remaining two rows are irrelevant since an opponent must fill the third square with an X or lose the game.

Silverman was delighted when he tallied up the final total of relevant boards: only 48. For each of them he noted the appropriate move by the machine. The surprisingly short list of possible board positions heartened Hillis. The group converged on Hot Springs, Silverman says, "with the list of 48 patterns and only a vague idea of how to interpret them mechanically."

(Readers who have a fanatical bent—or are stranded in airline terminals—may enjoy working out the game tree on a few sheets of paper. How long does it take, after all, to draw 48 tic-tac-toe patterns? Four symbols should help sort things out: X, O, blank and a dash for "don't care.")

Once settled in Hot Springs, the team assembled the raw material for their spool-and-stick odyssey: 30 boxes of Tinkertoys, each containing 250 pieces. Some team members put together the supporting framework that would hold all 48 memory spindles. To explain precisely how the spindles were made, I must digress for a moment and describe the conventions employed by the team to encode tic-tac-toe positions.

First, the squares of a tic-tac-toe board were numbered as follows:

$$1\ 2\ 3$$
$$4\ 5\ 6$$
$$7\ 8\ 9$$

Then a memory spindle was divided conceptually into nine consecutive lengths in which information about the status of each tic-tac-toe square was stored from left to right.

Each length was further subdivided into three equal sections, one for each possible item one might find in a square: an X, an O or a blank. Each possibility was encoded by the lack of a spool. For example, if an X happened to occupy a certain square, the memory spindle would have no spool in the first position, one spool in the second and one spool in the third. Similarly, a spool missing in the second position denoted an unplayed square, and one missing in the third position symbolized an O. Finally, if all three spools were missing, it meant that what occupied the square was irrelevant.

One can hardly mention the subject of memory spindles without bringing up the core piece, a thing of digital beauty. Here the Latin *digitus* came into its own, the construction resembling a kind of rotating claw with nine fingers. The core piece and a sample memory spindle are shown in Figure 1.3.

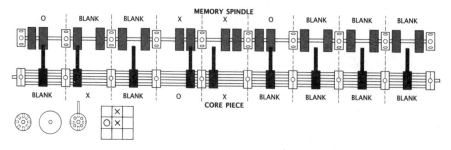

Figure 1.3 A memory spindle, which encodes the X's and O's of a tic-tac-toe board, prevents the core piece from turning.

The core piece consisted of nine equal sections. Each had its own finger, a short stick protruding from the rim of a sliding spool. Within each section the finger could be moved along the axis of the core piece into any of three possible positions: one for X, one for O and one for blank. The core piece could therefore store any possible tic-tac-toe board by virtue of the positions of its nine fingers as moved by the operator for each play by human or machine. In Figure 1.3, fingers in the consecutive positions 2, 1, 2, 3, 1, 2, 2, 2, 2 would represent the board shown.

If the current situation of play is stored in the core piece, does the Tinkertoy computer require any other memory? Could spool-and-stick logic devices be strung together to cogitate on the position and ultimately to signal a move? Well, yes — but such a Tinkertoy computer would be complicated and immense. The memory spindles eliminated the need for most of the computer's cogitation. All the Tinkertoy computer had to do was to look up the current board in the memory spindles. The only purpose of the search, naturally, was to decide what move to make.

A glance at Figure 1.1 makes it clear that each memory spindle was accompanied by a number written on a paper strip hanging next to its output duck. These numbers were the machine's responses. As the read head clicks down the rows of spindles, the core piece wants to turn but cannot as long as at least one memory-spindle spool blocks one of the core piece's nine fingers. Only when the read head falls adjacent to the spindle that matches the current board do all nine fingers miss. Then the core piece whirls.

By a mechanism that would do Rube Goldberg proud, a stick protruding from the end of the core piece engages another stick connected to the output duck. The spinning core piece thus kicks the duck off its perch to peck at a number writ large on the paper strip.

Computer purists will ask whether the Tinkertoy contraption really deserves the title "computer." It is not, to be sure, programmable in the usual sense: one cannot sit at a keyboard and type in a program for it to follow. On the other hand, one could certainly change the memory spindles, albeit with some difficulty, and thus reprogram the computer for other games. Imagine a Tinkertoy device that plays *go–moku narabe* (a game played on an 11-by-11 board in which one player tries to place five black stones in a row while preventing an opponent from creating a row of five white stones). A Tinkertoy computer programmed for *go–moku narabe*, however, would probably tower into the stratosphere.

The real lesson the Tinkertoy computer can teach us resides in a rather amazing feature of digital computation: at the very root of a computation lies merely an essential flow of information. The computer hardware itself can take on many forms and designs. One could build perfectly accurate computers not only of Tinkertoys but also of bamboo poles, ropes and pulleys (as in Chapter 2), plastic tubes and water — even, strange to think, electrical components. The last-named are preferred, of course, because of their speed. It would be short-sighted indeed to sneer at a computer made of Tinkertoys merely because it is not electronic. After all, even electrons and wires may not be the best materials for quick computer processing. Photons and fibers are gaining on them fast.

Actually, Tinkertoys are well suited to digital computing. For example, the memory spindles use a binary principle: the presence or absence of spools denotes the status of a particular square on a tic-tac-toe board. The core piece exhibits digital logic: it can turn only if all its fingers miss corresponding spools on a memory spindle. Such an operation is called "and." One can trace the logic for the core piece in Figure 1.3: if the first spool is absent from the first section of the memory spindle *and* the second spool is absent from the second section *and* the third spool is absent from the third section *and* so on — only if all nine conditions are met will the core piece turn. The beauty of the Tinkertoy computer is not just its clever mechanics but its subtle logic.

Tinkertoy purists will be happy to know that the M.I.T. students stuck to the original wooden sticks and spools with only a few exceptions (see Figure 1.4). An occasional aluminum rod runs through the framework to strengthen it. Two wire cables, an axle and a crank transmit motive power to the awesome machine for its next move. Finally, the very joints of sticks and spools were made firm by glue and escutcheon pins —pieces of hardware that commonly hold commemorative plaques in place. The team inserted the pins in holes drilled through the rim of the spool down to the original, central hole and through its stick — a task they had to repeat more than 1,000 times. (When Hillis walked into a hardware store to obtain several thousand escutcheon pins, the manager looked bewildered. "We have," Hillis said with a straight face, "a lot of escutcheons.")

The Tinkertoy tic-tac-toe computer suffered the fate of most museum exhibits. It was taken apart and crated. At latest report, it was sitting in storage at the Mid-America Center, waiting to reemerge, perhaps,

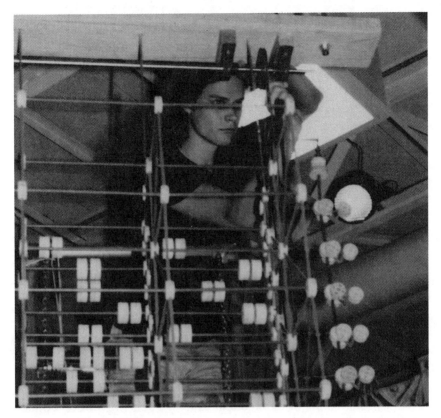

Figure 1.4 Edward Hardebeck helps to assemble the Tinkertoy computer.

into the limelight. It may yet click its way to victory after victory, a monument to the Tinkertoy dreams of childhood.

Further Reading

Charles Babbage et al. *Charles Babbage: On the Principles and Development of the Calculator and Other Seminal Writings.* Philip Morrison and Emily Morrison, eds. Dover Publications, 1961.

Sing H. Lee and Ravindra A. Athale, eds. *Optical Computing.* Special issue of *Optical Engineering,* Vol. 28, No. 4 (April 1989).

2

The Rope-and-Pulley Wonder

The Apraphulian excursion fooled few people when it
first appeared in *Scientific American* in April, 1988.

A. K. DEWDNEY, *The Magic Machine*

On the island of Apraphul off the northwest coast of New Guinea, archaeologists have discovered the rotting remnants of an ingenious arrangement of ropes and pulleys thought to be the first working digital computer ever constructed. Chief investigator Robert L. Ripley of Charles Fort College in New York dates the construction to approximately A.D. 850.

The Apraphulians were excellent sailors. Their ships were wonderfully built and equipped with the most elaborate rigging imaginable. Were the Apraphulians led to the digital computer by their mastery of rope or was it the other way around? Experts continue to debate the topic hotly.

The ancient rope-and-pulley computer has been partially reconstructed by Ripley and his team at the Tropical Museum of Marine Antiquities in nearby Sumatra. Scouring a site that extends through several kilometers of dense jungle east of the Pulleg Mountains, the group found faint traces of buried jute fibers and noted the exact position of badly corroded brass pulleys and associated hardware. The reconstruction has given me an ideal opportunity to introduce readers to the principles of digital computing without resorting to tiny and mysterious electronic components. Here are gates, flip-flops, and circuits made entirely of rope and pulleys. It is all visible and perfectly easy to understand.

The Apraphulians used a binary system just as we do, but the numbers 0 and 1 were represented by the positions of ropes instead of by electric voltages. Imagine a black blox with a hole drilled in one side. The reader holds a taut rope that passes through the hole. This position of the rope represents the digit 0. If the reader now pulls on the rope, a creak and squeal inside the box is heard as a foot or so of rope comes out. The new position of the rope represents the digit 1.

One can represent numbers with such boxes. Any number from 0 through 7, for instance, can be represented by three boxes (Figure 2.1). By employing more boxes, larger numbers can be represented. Ten boxes suffice to represent all numbers from 0 through 1023.

My example of the black box is not arbitrary. The Apraphulians apparently loved to enclose their mechanisms in black wood boxes, small and large. It may be that the construction of computers was the prerogative of a special technological priesthood. The sight of great assemblages of black boxes may have kept the masses trembling in awe.

One of the key devices used by the Apraphulians converted a 0 into a 1 and a 1 into a 0. (It is occasionally convenient to speak of 0 and 1 instead of "in" and "out.") Akin to what modern computer engineers call an inverter, this interesting mechanism consisted of a box with a hole drilled in its front and another in its back (Figure 2.2). When someone (or something) pulled the input rope at the front of the box, an equal amount of output rope would be played out of the hole in the back. On

BOX 1	BOX 2	BOX 3	NUMBER
IN	IN	IN	0
IN	IN	OUT	1
IN	OUT	IN	2
IN	OUT	OUT	3
OUT	IN	IN	4
OUT	IN	OUT	5
OUT	OUT	IN	6
OUT	OUT	OUT	7

Figure 2.1 How Apraphulians represented numbers.

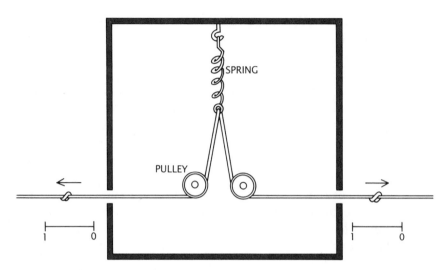

Figure 2.2 The Apraphulian inverter.

peering into the box, the reason is obvious: The ropes entering the box
from front and back pass over two fixed pulleys toward one side of the
box, where they attach to a single spring.

As some readers may have surmised already, the digits 0 and 1 were
not encoded so much by "out" and "in" as they were by the direction in
which the rope moved. The point is best illustrated by a box that has no
mechanism in it whatever. A piece of rope enters a single hole in the
front of the box and leaves by a single hole in the back. If one pulls the
rope from the 0 position to the 1 position at the front of the box, the rope
moves from "in" to "out." The direction of movement is toward the
puller. The rope simultaneously moves from "out" to "in" at the back of
the box, but since the direction of movement is still toward the puller,
the rope at the back of the box also moves from 0 to 1.

Two additional mechanisms almost complete the ancient Apraphulian repertoire of computing components. The first mechanism had two
input ropes entering a box. If either rope was in the 1 position, the single
output rope would also be in the 1 position. The Apraphulians managed
this trick by absurdly simple means (Figure 2.3). Each rope entering the
front of the box passed over a pair of pulleys that brought it close to the
other rope. The two ropes, passing toward the rear of the box, were then
tied to a single ring linked to the output rope. If either or both of the input
ropes were pulled, the ring would be pulled directly. Because the output

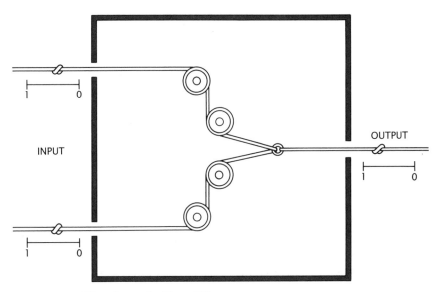

Figure 2.3 The Apraphulian OR gate.

of the box was 1 if one input *or* the other was 1, today's engineers would call this an OR gate.

The ancient Apraphulians fabricated what we would call an AND gate from four pulleys and a spring (Figure 2.4). The two input ropes, in reality the same rope, passed over three of the pulleys, two of which acted as guides. The third pulley acted as a numerical divider; if one pulled one input rope by the amount x, the third pulley would move toward the front of the box by the amount $\frac{1}{2}x$. If x should happen to be one unit, indicating an input of 1, nothing would happen at the output end owing to a curious linkage between the third pulley and a fourth one situated in the back of the box. The third pulley was attached to the fourth by means of two rods (ropes would do equally well) joined by a weak spring. When the third pulley moved $\frac{1}{2}$ unit toward the front of the box, the spring would extend and a parallel rope of $\frac{1}{2}$ unit length would tighten to take up the slack. If the other input rope were now pulled into the 1 position, the third and fourth pulleys would move in unison $\frac{1}{2}$ unit toward the front of the box. Since the fourth pulley acted as a two-multiplier, multiplying any forward motion by 2 in terms of its associated output rope, the ensemble would convert the second 1 input into an output of 1.

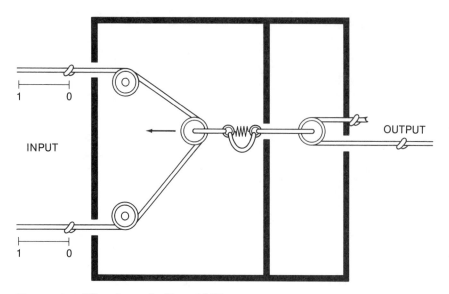

Figure 2.4 The Apraphulian AND gate.

The name AND gate is derived from the fact that the output of this device is 1 if and only if one input rope *and* the other are in position 1.

With these components one can build all the control circuits of a digital computer. These include circuits that compute arithmetic functions, interpret program code, and direct the flow of information among the parts of the computer.

Did the Apraphulians construct their computer along such lines? The evidence is too fragmentary to reach a definitive conclusion, but archaeo-computologists working with Ripley maintain they have discovered a simple multiplexer within the half-buried complex. In electronic computers a multiplexer is essentially an electrical switch that directs the passage of many signals through a single wire. For example, the simplest multiplexer would have two input wires we might label a and b. At any given moment each wire could carry a 0 or 1 signal. Which of the two signals, a or b, will be allowed to pass through the device and out a single output wire d? The answer to that question is the business of a control wire, c; if it carries a 1 signal, the signal from wire a will be transmitted along the output wire. If the control wire carries a 0, on the other hand, the signal in wire b will be transmitted (Figure 2.5).

This reconstructed double-input Apraphulian multiplexer consists of two AND gates, an OR gate and an inverter. The whole thing is so sim-

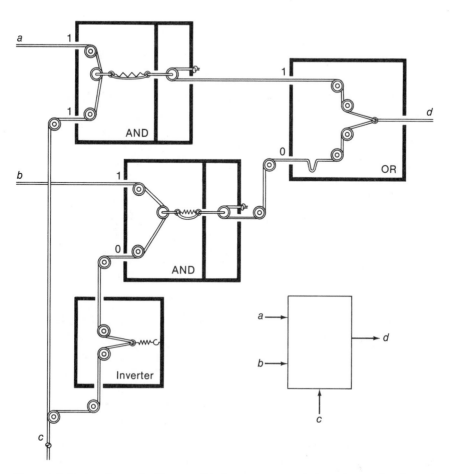

Figure 2.5 An Apraphulian multiplexer: rope c determines whether signals from a or b reach d.

ple that one dares to believe computer recreationists might build their own Apraphulian multiplexer at home. Hardware stores might suffer a puzzling run on rope and pulleys. In any event, one can follow operations of the multiplexer by referring to Figure 2.5. Ropes a and b enter the multiplexer from the top left, each going to its own AND gate. Rope c is split. One branch runs directly to the other input port of the AND gate to which rope a goes. The second branch of rope c passes through an inverter and then runs to the AND gate to which rope b goes. If rope c is pulled to a value of 1 and held, any sequence of 0's and 1's sent along rope a will be faithfully transmitted through the upper AND gate and on to the OR gate. At the same time any signal sent along rope b will be stopped at the lower AND gate. If rope c is relaxed to its 0 position, the inverter creates a 1 at the lower AND gate. In this case any signal sent along rope b will now be transmitted through the lower AND gate and signals on rope a will be ignored.

The OR gate merely ties the two output signals together, so to speak. If the signal from rope a is currently being transmitted, one can easily visualize exactly what happens directly from the diagram: If rope a is relaxed to the 0 position, the rear pulley in the AND box moves toward the rear of the box. A 0 is thus transmitted along the output rope and into the OR box. The other input rope to this box is already in the 0 position (slack). The natural tension on the output rope d immediately pulls it into the new position, namely 0. If one pulls on rope a again, the pull is transmitted along the path that has just been described, with the result that rope d is retracted.

The matter of slack ropes compels me to take up the question of tension in the Apraphulian computer. Sometimes, as in the OR gate of the example, a rope will become slack. There is naturally a danger that such ropes will slip right off their pulleys. Ripley tells me that in such cases the Apraphulians used a specially modified inverter with an extremely weak spring to remedy the problem. Wherever a rope was likely to develop slack, a "weak inverter" was installed to maintain the minimum tension associated with the signal 0.

No general-purpose computer is complete without a memory. The memory of the Apraphulian computer consisted of hundreds of special storage elements we would call flip-flops. Here again the remarkable simplicity of the Apraphulian mind is immediately evident. In line with modern terminology, the two ropes entering the mechanical flip-flop are labeled set and reset (Figure 2.6). The two ropes were connected over a series of three pulleys in such a way that when the set rope was pulled away from the box into the 1 position, the reset rope would be pulled toward the box into the 0 position. The common rope was connected to a sliding bar at the back of the flip-flop box. The output rope, physically a continuation of the set rope, had a large bead attached to it that engaged a slot in the sliding bar. As the set rope was pulled, the bead rode over the end of the bar, popping into the slot when the set rope reached the end of its travel. In this position, 1 was "remembered."

As a consequence the output rope was held in position until the enormous rope computer changed things by pulling on the reset rope. That

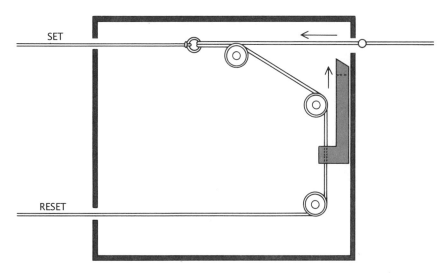

Figure 2.6 The Apraphulian flip-flop served as a memory element.

had the effect of pulling the sliding bar away from the bead, releasing it and playing the output rope into the 0 position. In this case the flip-flop would henceforth "remember" 0. How were such memory elements used in the Apraphulian computer?

Ripley and his team were puzzled to discover in the midst of the vast Apraphulian computer complex a large overgrown field nearly a kilometer wide. Buried just below the surface of the field were several thousand rotting flip-flop boxes arranged in rows of eight. Ripley, with the aid of the archaeocomputologists, eventually surmised that the field represented the Apraphulian computer's main memory. Each row of eight boxes would have constituted a single, eight-bit "word" in the same sense that the three boxes of my earlier example would have constituted a three-bit word. In that vein, imagine a row of three flip-flops that had been set to the values 1, 0, and 1. They would have stored the number 5.

The content of this particular memory word would have been accessed by the rope-and-pulley computer as follows. Each flip-flop in the row would send an output rope to an associated AND box. The other input to each AND box would come from a special rope used to retrieve the contents of the word in question. When the ropes were pulled, the outputs of the AND boxes would be identical with the outputs of the flip-flops. The AND box ropes would lead to a large assemblage of OR boxes and thence into a special array of flip-flops we would call a register. A single tug on the rope associated with the word under examination would place the same binary pattern of rope positions in the register.

The computer's main logic unit undoubtedly would have directed the flow of information not just from memory to registers but between registers as well. In particular, by the use of multiplexers and demultiplexers (which perform the opposite function of multiplexers), the computer would have sent patterns from register to register. At a specific register that we would call the arithmetic register, patterns would have been combined according to the rules of addition and multiplication.

The Apraphulian computer is believed to have been programmable. If it was, part of its vast memory would have been used to store the program. Program instructions would also have been merely patterns of 0's and 1's retrieved by the same mechanism outlined earlier. Those patterns would in due course have been sent to an instruction register for interpretation by the computer's logic unit.

It is a pity I can do little more in these pages than to hint at the marvelous complexity of the Apraphulian machine. It must have been an amazing sight when in operation. Because of the enormous lengths of rope involved, no human being would have had the strength to pull the input levers into the appropriate positions. The presence of elephant bones in the Apraphulian complex makes the source of input power immediately clear. At the output end large springs maintained appropriate tensions in the system. Perhaps flags on the ultimate output ropes enabled members of the technological priesthood to read the outcome of whatever computation was in progress.

The Apraphulian rope-and-pulley computer makes for an interesting contrast with the recently proposed nanocomputer (see Further Reading). The rope machine, of course, inhabits a distant past, whereas the nanometer-scale machine dwells in a hazy future. The Apraphulian computer is relatively massive in scale, covering thousands of acres; the nanocomputer is incredibly tiny, occupying an area one-thousandth the size of a human cell nucleus. The mere concept of either machine serves as a springboard into a speculative realm where recreation blends with science. Think, for example, of the ongoing dream of artificially intelligent machines. We find it easier to accept the possibility of an electronic computer that thinks since our own thoughts are to a great extent electronically mediated. Because any modern computer (and its program) is conceptually translatable into Apraphulian form, any artificially intelligent device ever realized now or in the future will have its rope-and-pulley counterpart. Can we imagine HAL 9000, the paranoid computer in

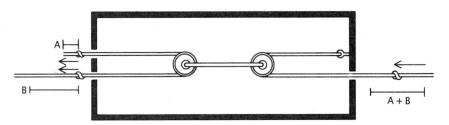

Figure 2.7 An Apraphulian adding machine.

the movie *2001: A Space Odyssey*, being so constructed? Are we willing to admit that an enormous building full of ropes and pulleys could be just as smart as we are? (For a partial answer, see Chapter 3.)

We leave the island of Apraphul with just one backward glance at its misty past: How might the vast digital computer have evolved? From analog ones, of course. Figure 2.7 shows an analog adding machine made from two ropes and two pulleys. The two ends of one rope enter the front of a box through two holes. The rope passes over a single pulley that is linked with another pulley by an axial connector. One end of the second rope is attached to the back of the box. The rope passes over the second pulley and then through a hole in the back of the box. Readers might find some diversion in discovering for themselves how the machine adds two numbers; if the two input ropes are pulled a distance a and b respectively, the output rope travels a distance $a + b$.

So much is clear. But how did the Apraphulians manage analog multiplication?

Further Reading

A. K. Dewdney, "Atomic Computers," in *The Magic Machine*, W. H. Freeman, 1990.

3

THE INFINITE BRAIN

"Are minds subject to the laws of physics? What,
indeed, *are* the laws of physics?"

ROGER PENROSE, *The Emperor's New Mind*

Human intelligence outstrips artificial intelligence because it exploits physics at the quantum-mechanical level. That is a provocative position, but one that Roger Penrose, the noted mathematical physicist, leans toward in his book, *The Emperor's New Mind.* Although (as Penrose readily admits) the proposition cannot be rigorously proved at present, the intriguing arguments in *The Emperor's New Mind* have produced some healthy doubts about the philosophical foundations of artificial intelligence.

I shall present Penrose's arguments — but because this book follows its own compass in charting unknown waters, I shall challenge some of his conclusions and tinker with some of his ideas. In particular, I shall expand the question How do people think? to ask whether human beings will ever know enough to answer such a question. If the universe has an infinite structure, humans may never answer the question fully. An infinite regress of structure, on the other hand, offers some unique computational opportunities.

Before jumping into such matters, I invite readers to explore the recesses of *The Emperor's New Mind* with me. First, we shall visit the famed Chinese room to inquire whether "intelligent" programs understand what they are doing. Next, a brief tour of the Platonic pool hall will bring us face to face with a billiards table that exploits the classical physics of elastic collisions to compute practically anything. Moving along to Erwin Schrödinger's laboratory, we shall inquire after the health of his cat in order to investigate the relation between classical physics and quantum mechanics. Finally, we shall reach our destination: an infinite intelligence able to solve a problem that no ordinary, finite computer could ever hope to conquer.

Watching television one evening several years ago, Penrose felt drawn to a BBC program in which proponents of artificial intelligence made what seemed to be a brash claim. They maintained that computers, more or less in their present form, could some day be just as intelligent as humans—perhaps even more so. The claim irritated Penrose. How could the complexities of human intelligence, especially creativity, arise from an algorithm churning away within a computer brain? The extremity of the claims "goaded" him into the project that led to *The Emperor's New Mind*.

A methodical exploration of computing theory brought Penrose to criticize one of its philosophical cornerstones, the Turing test. Many computer scientists accept the test as a valid way of distinguishing an intelligent program from a nonintelligent one. In the test, a human interrogator types messages to two hidden subjects, one a person and the other a computer programmed to respond to questions in an intelligent manner. If, after a reasonable amount of time, the interrogator cannot tell the difference between the typed responses of the human and those of the computer, then the program has passed the Turing test.

Penrose argues that the test provides only indirect evidence for intelligence. After all, what may appear to be an intelligent entity may turn out to be a mockery, just as an object and its mirror image look identical but in other details are different. Penrose maintains that a direct method for measuring intelligence may require more than a simple Turing test.

To strengthen his argument, Penrose wanders into the Chinese room, a peculiar variation of the Turing test invented by philosopher John R. Searle. A human interrogator stands outside a room that only allows the entrance and exit of paper messages. The interrogator types out a story and related questions and sends them into the room. The twist: all messages that go into and out of the room are typed in Chinese characters.

To make matters even more bizarre, a person inside the room executes a program that responds to the story by answering questions about it. This person exactly replaces the computer hardware. The task would be tedious and boring but, once the rules of execution were learned, rather straightforward. To guarantee the ignorance of the human hardware, he or she has no knowledge whatsoever of Chinese. Yet the Chinese room seems to understand the story and responds to the questions intelligently.

The upshot of the exercise, as far as Penrose is concerned, is that "the mere carrying out of a successful algorithm does *not* in itself imply that any understanding has taken place." His conclusion certainly holds if it is directed at the executing apparatus, whether flesh or hardware. After all, whether the program happens to be executed by a human or by a computer makes no difference, in principle, to the outcome of the program's interaction with the outside world.

But for this very reason the human in the Chinese room is something of a straw man: no one would fault a program because the hardware fails to understand what the program is all about. To put the point even more strongly, no one would be critical of a neuron for not understanding the significance of the pulse patterns that come and go. This would be true whether or not the neuron happened to be executing part of an algorithm or doing something far more sophisticated. Any strength in claims for artificial intelligence must surely lie in the algorithm itself. And that is where Penrose attacks next.

The world of algorithms is essentially the world of the computable. In Penrose's words, algorithms constitute "a very narrow and limited part of mathematics." Penrose believes (as I and many other mathematicians do) in a kind of Platonic reality inhabited by mathematical objects. Our clue to the independent existence of such objects lies in our complete inability to change them. They are just "there," like mountains or oceans.

Penrose cites the Mandelbrot set as an example. The Mandelbrot set was not "invented" by Benoit B. Mandelbrot, the renowned IBM research fellow, but was discovered by him. Like the planet Neptune, the set existed long before any human set eyes on it and recognized its significance. The Mandelbrot set carries an important message for those who imagine it to be a creature of the computer. It is not. The Mandelbrot set cannot even be computed! Do I hear howls of outrage? Strictly speaking, Penrose is right.

The Mandelbrot set, while it is but one landmark in the Platonic world, lies somewhat distant from algorithmic explorers. Readers may recall that points in the interior of the set can be found by an iterative process: a complex number c is squared and then the result, z_1, is squared and added to c, then the second result, z_2, is squared and added to c and so on. If the succession of z values thus produced never patters off into infinity, then c belongs to the set's interior. But here a grave question emerges. How long does one have to wait to decide whether the sequence of values remains bounded? The answer is, essentially, forever (Figure 3.1)!

In practice one interposes a cutoff to the computation. In doing so one inevitably includes a few points that do not belong in the set because it takes longer for the sequence based on such points to diverge. Difficulties in computing the Mandelbrot set pale in comparison with other limitations on the algorithmic adventure. For example, mathematics itself is formally considered to be built of axiom systems. Set forth a modest collection of axioms, a rule of inference or two — and one is in business. A conceptual algorithm called the British Museum Algorithm generates all the theorems that are provable within the formal systems of axioms and inference rules. Unfortunately, the theorems thus produced do not necessarily include all truths of the system.

This discovery, by the mathematician Kurt Gödel, dashed hopes of mechanizing all of mathematics. Penrose takes Gödel's famous theorem as evidence that human intelligence can transcend the algorithmic method: ". . . a clear consequence of the Gödel argument [is] that the

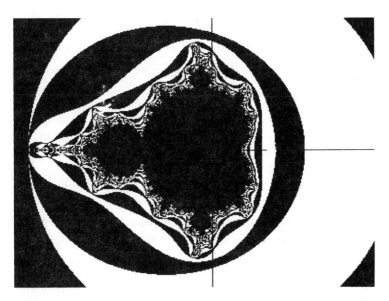

Figure 3.1 The Mandelbrot set amid a field of contour lines.

concept of mathematical truth cannot be encapsulated in any formal scheme." How then could Gödel's theorem itself be the result of an algorithm?

As a theorem, Gödel's result is itself completely formalizable. It can be derived, in principle, by a systematic theorem generator from the appropriate axioms and rules of inference. Penrose really should have stopped to think of that.

Whatever one's opinion on such questions, *The Emperor's New Mind* attacks the claims of artificial intelligence on another front: the physics of computing. Penrose hints that the real home of computing lies more in the tangible world of classical mechanics than in the imponderable realm of quantum mechanics. The modern computer is a deterministic system that for the most part simply executes algorithms. In a somewhat jolly fashion, Penrose takes a billiard table, the scene of so many classical encounters, as the appropriate framework for a computer in the classical mold.

By reconfiguring the boundaries of a billiard table, one might make a computer in which the billiard balls act as message carriers and their interactions act as logical decisions. The billiard-ball computer was first designed some years ago by the computer scientists Edward Fredkin and Tommaso Toffoli of the Massachusetts Institute of Technology. The reader can appreciate the simplicity and power of a billiard-ball computer by examining Figure 3.2.

The diagram depicts a billiard-ball logic device. Two in-channels admit moving balls into a special chamber, which has three out-channels. If just one ball enters the chamber from either in-channel, it will leave by either the bottom out-channel or the one at the upper right. If two balls enter the chamber at the same time, however, one of them will leave by the out-channel at the lower right. The presence or absence of a ball in this particular out-channel signals the logical function known as an AND gate. The output is a ball if, and only if, a ball enters both one in-channel *and* the other one.

A computer can be built out of this particular gate type and just one other, a chamber in which a ball leaves by a particular channel if, and only if, a ball does not enter by another channel. Readers may enjoy trying to design such a chamber, bearing in mind that additional balls might be helpful in the enterprise.

Everyone appreciates the smooth, classical motions of a billiard ball. It has other desirable properties that are hardly given a second thought. For example, no one ever has to worry whether a billiard ball is in two

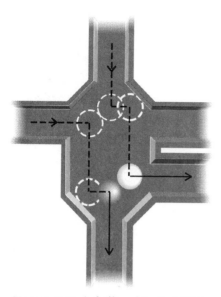

Figure 3.2 A billiard-ball AND gate.

places at the same time. Quantum mechanics, however, produces such anxieties. Quantum systems such as the famous two-slit experiment leave open the possibility that a photon can be in two places at once.

Briefly, when photons pass through a double slit, they can be regarded as waves that interfere with themselves. An interference pattern emerges on a screen behind the slits unless one places a detector at either slit. The act of observation forces the photon to decide, in effect, which hole it will pass through! The phenomenon is called a state vector collapse. The experiment can be extended to an observation that takes place at either of two sites that are a kilometer (even a light-year) apart. The photon can decide which slit it will pass through, many physicists claim, only if it is effectively in both places at once.

At what point in the continuum of scales, from the atomic to the galactic, does a quantum-mechanical system become a classical one? The dilemma is illustrated by Schrödinger's famous cat in Figure 3.3. In this *gedanken* (thought) experiment, a scientist who has no fear of animal-rights activists places a cat and a vial of toxic gas in a room that contains a laser, a half-silvered mirror, a light detector, and a hammer.

When the room is sealed, the laser emits a photon toward the mirror. If the photon passes through the mirror, no harm comes to the cat. But if the photon is reflected in the mirror, it hits the detector, which activates

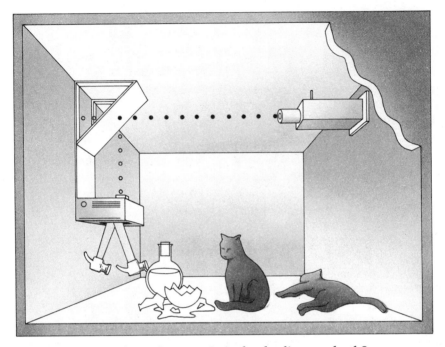

Figure 3.3 Schrödinger's cat—is it dead, alive, or both?

the hammer, which smashes the vial, which contains the gas, which kills the cat. From outside the room one cannot know whether the cat lives or dies.

In the quantum-mechanical world, the two possible events coexist as superposed realities. But in the classical world, only one event or the other may occur. The state vector (and possibly the cat) must collapse. Penrose suggests that current theory lacks a way of treating the middle ground between classical physics and quantum mechanics. The theory is split in two but should be seamless on a grand scale. Perhaps the synthesis will come from an area known as quantum gravity.

Now back, finally, to the human mind. For Penrose, consciousness has a nonalgorithmic ingredient. At the quantum level, different alternatives can coexist. A single quantum state could in principle consist of a large number of different, simultaneous activities. Is the human brain somehow able to exploit this phenomenon? I can hardly explore this eerie possibility as well as Penrose does. Readers intrigued by the thought had best buy the book.

I was inspired, however, to investigate a related question. Could human beings quantify their own intelligence in a universe whose structure goes on forever? An end to the structure of matter, either as an ultimate particle or a set of particles, seems inconceivable. By this I mean not just particles but any structure, whether energetic or even purely informational, underlying the phenomena in question.

It seems to me that physics itself may be an infinite enterprise for the simple reason that as soon as some "ultimate" structure is discovered, explaining the existence of the "ultimate" laws becomes the next problem. In any event, I would prefer to live in an infinitely structured universe. For one thing, our minds might turn out to be much more powerful than if the structure went only so far.

Computers are constructed to rule out the influence of any physical process below a certain scale of size. The algorithm must be protected from "errors." Our brains may or may not be so structured, as Penrose points out. Physical events at the atomic level might well have an important role to play in thought formation. Processes at the molecular level certainly do. One has only to think of the influence of neurotransmitter molecules on the behavior of a neuron. Furthermore, it is a well-known characteristic of nature to take advantage of physical possibilities in the deployment of biological operations. If physical structures extend to a certain level, is there some a priori reason to believe that the brain must automatically be excluded from exploiting it?

What if the brain could exploit all levels of structure in an infinitely structured universe? To demonstrate in the crudest imaginable way the potential powers of an infinite brain, I have designed an infinite computer that exploits the structure at all levels. For the purposes of the demonstration, I will pretend that the structure is classical at all scales.

My infinite computer (Figure 3.4) is essentially a square that contains two rectangles and two other, smaller squares. An input wire enters the big square from the left and passes immediately into the first rectangle. This represents a signal-processing device that I shall call a substitution module. The substitution module sends a wire to each of the two small squares and also to the other rectangle, henceforth called a message module.

The structure of the whole computer regresses infinitely. Each of the two smaller squares is an exact duplicate of the large square, but at half the scale. When a signal is propagated through the wires and modules at half the scale, it takes only half as long to traverse the distances involved,

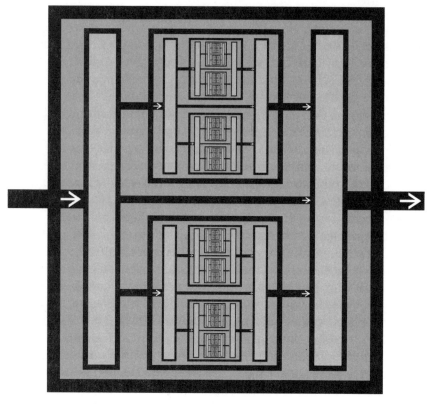

Figure 3.4 A fractal computer solves Thue's word problem.

and so the substitution and message modules operate twice as fast as the corresponding modules one level up.

The infinite computer solves the famous "word problem" invented by the mathematician Axel Thue. In this problem, one is given two words and a dictionary of allowed substitutions. Can one, by substitutions alone, get from the first word to the second one? Here is an example of the problem: suppose the first "word" is 100101110 and the second is 01011101110. Can one change the first word into the second by substituting 010 for 110, 10 for 111, and 100 for 001? The example is chosen at random. I deliberately refrain from attempting to solve it.

It might happen that no sequence of substitutions will transform the first word into the second. On the other hand, there might be a sequence of substitutions that does the job. In the course of these substitutions, intermediate words might develop that are very long. Therein lies the problem. As with certain points in the Mandelbrot set, one cannot effectively decide the answer. There is no algorithm for the problem, because an algorithm must terminate, by definition. The danger is that the algorithm might terminate before the question is decided. Thue's word problem is called undecidable for this reason. No computer program, even in principle, can solve all instances of this problem.

Enter the infinite computer. The target word is given to the computer through the main input wire. It enters the first substitution module in ¼ second. The word is then transmitted by the substitution module to the two substitution modules at the next level. But this transmission takes only ⅛ second. Transmission to subsequent levels takes 1/16, then 1/32 second, and so on. The total time for all substitution modules to become "loaded" with the target word is therefore half a second.

Next, the three (or however many) substitution formulas are fed into the computer by the same process and at the same speed. This time, however, the various substitution modules at different levels are preprogrammed to accept only certain substitutions in the sequence as their own, and they are also preprogrammed always to attempt a substitution at a specific place in a word that arrives from a higher level. A recital of the distribution scheme for farming out the substitutions and their places would probably try the reader's patience, and so I shall omit it. This should not prevent those who enjoy infinite excursions from imagining how it might be managed.

The computation begins when one sends the first word into the computer. The first substitution module attempts to make its own substitution at its allotted place in the incoming word. If the substitution cannot be made in the required place, the substitution module transmits the word to the lower square in the next level inward; if it succeeds in making the substitution, it transmits the transformed word to the upper square. If the substitution succeeds *and* the newly produced word matches the target word stored in the substitution module's memory, then the module sends a special signal to the message module: "success."

Each square at each level operates exactly in this manner. As I indicated earlier, it is possible to distribute substitutions (and places at which they are to be attempted) throughout the infinite computer in such a way that the word problem will always be solved. The question takes at most one second to decide in all cases: half a second for the computation to proceed all the way down to infinitesimal modules and half a second for the message "success" to reach the main output wire. If no substitution sequence exists, the absence of a message after one second may be taken as a "no" answer. Readers may enjoy pondering the infinite computer while exploiting the many (perhaps infinite) structures of their own brains.

Further Reading

Roger Penrose. *The Emperor's New Mind: Concerning Computers, Minds, and the Laws of Physics.* Oxford University Press, 1989.
Robert A. Wilson. *Schrödinger's Cat Trilogy.* Dell, 1988.

INVASION OF THE INSECTOIDS

As Gregor Samsa awoke one morning from uneasy dreams he found himself transformed in his bed into a gigantic insect.

FRANZ KAFKA, *The Metamorphosis*

Will the next major advance in robotics spring forth from inexpensive machines that crawl, think, and act like bugs? Researchers in the "insect lab" at the Massachusetts Institute of Technology hope so. They have spawned a swarm of small robots that behave like your average arthropod. These insectoids, as I call them, are based on new principles of robot design and threaten a paradigm shift in the field of robotics.

Until recently, engineers bent on designing a robotic "brain" have taken a determinedly analytic approach. In this traditional view, they first decide what the robot will be able to sense; they then consider how it will analyze sensory inputs and finally how it will plan and take action. Each step is fraught with complexities that are likely to bog down intricate projects.

Abandoning the traditional approach, Rodney Brooks, director of the insect lab, has adopted a design philosophy that he calls subsumption architecture. To apply this philosophy, he starts by designing a network of processors and hardware that can produce a simple behavior. No behavior is added to the system until the behavior it subsumes is up and running (or walking, as the case may be).

For instance, to design an artificial creature that wanders and avoids obstacles, Brooks would first assemble a creature that moved randomly and then add the detectors and processors that would sense objects and instruct the creature to change direction. In subsumption architecture, complex behaviors evolve from a variety of simple features.

To test the practicality of subsumption architecture, Brooks and a team of his graduate students began building and designing many insectoids, from Allen, a primitive robot on wheels, to Squirt, a delicate bug no bigger than a grasshopper. But no creature illustrates subsumption architecture as well as Genghis, a foot-long assembly of motors, struts, gears and microchips.

Genghis, who was created in part by graduate student Colin Angle, has six stiltlike legs, two whiskers and six infrared "eyes" transplanted from burglar alarms. Each leg is operated by a pair of motors (Figure 4.1). An Alpha Motor moves the leg forward or back; a Beta Motor swings the leg up and away from the body or moves it down and toward the body. Between Genghis's legs are microchips that serve as the insectoid's nerve center. The microchips contain numerous augmented finite-state machines (AFSMs). Each AFSM stores numerical information for controlling various aspects of Genghis's behavior, such as the movement of legs. The information, or state, of an AFSM may change from time to time, depending on the input it receives from other modules. The state will also determine how it reacts to the inputs.

Figure 4.1 A robotic insect named Genghis is a walking test bed of subsumption architecture. It can avoid obstacles and stalk people.

A robot must walk before it can run. In fact, to do anything worthwhile, Genghis must first stand up. Two numbers sent to the AFSMs control the Alpha and Beta Motors on each leg. One AFSM, called Alphapos, controls the Alpha Motor, and the other AFSM, Betapos, governs the Beta Motor. Each number represents vertical and lateral leg positions when Genghis is standing. As soon as Genghis is powered up in this simplest of behavioral settings, the motors all run until the leg positions (monitored by sensors) match the numbers stored in Alphapos and Betapos. The simple act constitutes what might be called the zero level of Genghis's architecture.

The next level of behavior, simple walking, is a feat robotics researchers have traditionally judged to be technically difficult. Genghis's basic walking network, in its simplest form, consists of two master AFSMs and 30 auxiliary ones, five per leg. Because the circuits for each of the insectoid's six legs are essentially the same, I will describe what happens to one leg and the five AFSMs that control it (Figure 4.2).

The key to basic walking is the global controller called Alpha Balance. This AFSM receives continual reports, in the form of numbers, on the positions of all six legs. A positive number indicates that a leg is pointing forward; a negative number, that it is pointing backward. Not surprisingly, legs that point straight out from the body are represented by zero. Alpha Balance adds these numbers together, the sum being a kind of average. If the sum is positive, it means that on average the legs are pointing forward. If the sum is negative, the average leg projects rearward.

The whole trick to walking revolves around the fact that if five of the legs touch the ground and a sixth is raised, then the insectoid may glide forward by a small amount merely by swinging all its ground legs slightly to the rear. If the insectoid then swings the upraised leg forward and places it gingerly back on the ground, it is one small step for an insectoid but one giant leap for robotics.

When Ghengis swings a leg to the front, Alpha Balance generates a sum that is positive and then sends a negative signal to all legs that are currently down. Their motors whine briefly, the insectoid moves forward a bit and the signal is rebalanced. That is all the Alpha-Balance Module cares about.

The manner in which the various modules interact to create the act of walking amounts to an electronic ballet among the modules of the six leg networks. The action begins for a particular leg when its Up-Leg Module is activated. The activation sets off a chain of coordinated

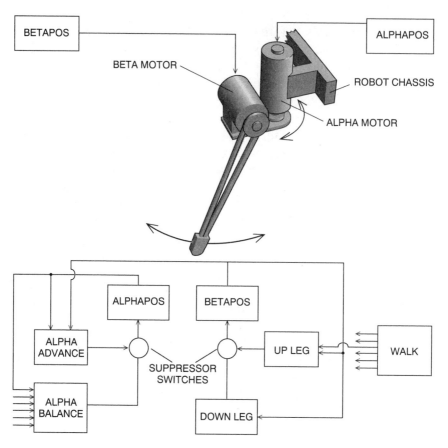

Figure 4.2 Basic circuitry that allows Genghis to stand (*top*) and walk (*bottom*).

events among the modules; the Up-Leg Module then signals the Betapos Module, sending it a number that reflects an upraised leg position. The Betapos Module, which controls the Beta Motor, normally receives a positive number (that keeps the leg firmly planted) from another module called Down Leg. The new, negative signal from the Up-Leg Module suppresses the positive signal from Down Leg. Consequently, the Beta Motor raises the leg to a point where its reported position matches the new signal.

This event triggers a completion state in the Betapos Module, and it signals this state to three other modules: Alpha Advance, Up Leg and Down Leg. The Alpha-Advance Module, which controls the back-and-forth motion of the leg, sends a strongly positive signal to the Alphapos Module. The Alpha Motor whirs gently, and the leg waves forward, almost as if it were probing the air. When the Up-Leg Module receives the completion signal, its action is suppressed. When the Down-Leg Module gets the completion signal, it is activated, and the Beta Motor powers the leg down to terra firma.

A master module, called Walk, controls the entire movement by sending a sequence of signals to the six Up-Leg Modules. But what sequence should it use? The triggering pattern most commonly used by insects is called the alternating tripod gait. If the legs are labeled R for right and L for left, as well as numbered $1, 2, 3$ from front to back, the alternating tripods are the sets $R1, L2, R3$ and $L1, R2, L3$. In normal situations, an insect like a cockroach will lift the first set, $R1, L2, R3$, leaving the other set on the ground. This triangular stance gives stability to the cockroach as the first set of three legs swings forward to new positions. Then the other set can be raised and swung forward in the same way while the first set provides stability.

The Walk Module may send out a sequential version of this set of signals to the six Up-Leg Modules. Or it could send out the pattern sometimes used by stick insects: $R3, L1, R2, L3, R1, L2$. There are numerous possibilities for stable gait patterns.

Perhaps readers can figure out the gait of a millipede machine. If there are 1,000 legs on each side of an insectoid, devise a gait that will carry the creature forward without any leg getting dragged along by the body.

Using the primitive network just described, Genghis could walk but not very smoothly and not in the manner that Brooks describes as "robust." For one thing, Genghis wobbled excessively and could not clear obstacles of even moderate height. The addition of a few more kinds of AFSM provided a new level of subsumption architecture and a new degree of behavioral competence.

A Beta-Force Module monitors the high strain that develops in a Beta Motor when its leg has been set down in a position that supports too much of the creature's total weight. Genghis may have stepped on a five-centimeter rock, for example. The Beta-Balance Module for that leg senses the unusually high force and sends a zero message that suppresses the leg-down message and makes the offending leg "compliant." The leg, in other words, gives way a bit, and Genghis compensates for the high terrain under one of its legs.

But on sloping terrain, the downhill end of Genghis will take more force than the upper end, and the legs will become compliant, increasing the pitch even more. Correcting this problem required two Pitch Modules to monitor the outputs from a pitch-measuring device. The Pitch Modules send messages to inhibit whichever Beta-Balance Modules have become too compliant.

When Genghis encounters an obstacle while swinging one of its legs forward, a sensor on the motor picks up the additional strain and sends a message to an Alpha-Force Module. This AFSM then sends a signal to the Up-Leg Module, which then results in a higher leg lift.

Among the many sensors used by Genghis are two whiskers and six infrared sensors. The whiskers send their reports to a feeler module. If a whisker senses an obstacle, the feeler module resets the Up-Leg Module for one of the two front legs.

The infrared sensors introduce the next major level of subsumption. The sensors work in conjunction with a Prowl Module, which gives Genghis a somewhat sinister mode of behavior. In this mode, Genghis rests quietly until it detects infrared radiation from, for example, a nearby human ankle. When that happens, Genghis activates its Walk Module. The creature then begins to creep forward like some demented insect toward the hapless human. Of course, there is plenty of time to get out of its way, but if a Steer Module is added as well, Genghis can be relentless.

A few years ago, when a curious visitor saw the insectoid for the first time, he asked, "Is it a bug?"

"No," Brooks said, repeating an old programming joke. "It's a feature." For a while, Brooks insisted on calling the insectoid "Feature." But later a graduate student suggested "Genghis," which seemed more appropriate for a creature whose instincts were to stalk and conquer.

Later some new circuits were added to Genghis to test whether self-organizing behavior might emerge in the absence of a central control module like Walk. The results were impressive. The microchip ganglion associated with each leg was given the option of running its own experiments with a set of basic behaviors like lifting or lowering a leg or swinging it forward or back. Each experiment consisted of recording what the neighboring legs were doing, then trying one of the basic behaviors and checking whether the body fell down or not. Fascinating to watch, according to Brooks, the experimenting insectoid might sit for a while, legs waving in the air, next thrash for a bit, then begin to move forward with tentative steps. Within a minute and a half, the network always "learned" the alternating tripod gait!

The notion of autonomy dominates the subsumption approach to robotic architecture in the M.I.T. insect lab. Can a robot, no matter how small, be given a behavior that will enable it to survive in the real world for extended periods? The insectoid called Squirt will fit inside a one-inch cube. Too small for legs in the current state of insectoid technology, it features wheels, a single motor, a microprocessor, two lithium batteries and three sensors. It uses two microphones to listen for sounds and a single light sensor to gauge the amount of light available.

Squirt will survive, provided it does not get stepped on. For this reason, it has been programmed with several layers of behavior that were transferred electronically from a computer to its single microchip. Squirt hides in the dark while listening for sounds. If it hears nothing for a few minutes, it ventures out in the general direction of the most recently heard sound. After wandering for a while, it engages in a spiral search to find a new hiding place.

In this respect, Squirt resembles the vehicles imagined by the German scientist Valentino Braitenberg. The purpose of Braitenberg vehicles, among other things, was to illustrate the thesis that very complex behaviors could result from very simple control systems. The thesis has inspired more than one robotics enthusiast to build a behavioral vehicle. But it was Brooks and company, also intrigued in part by Braitenberg's vehicles, who succeeded first. Some might be willing to ascribe emotions such as fear or longing to the behavior of the neurally controlled vehicles. Is Squirt afraid of people? It certainly acts like it.

Graduate student Anita Flynn, who was part of the team that built Squirt, sees the future of robotics blossoming in even smaller insectoids she calls gnats. These creatures would be the size of real insects, not to mention gnats themselves. Their body parts would be fabricated by the same techniques currently used to etch microcircuits on silicon surfaces. The biggest bottleneck is the ultratiny motors that gnats will require. The field of microengineering has already produced gears that would scatter at a sneeze. In the meantime, Brooks and company have built Attila, a more sophistocated version of Genghis (Figure 4.3).

Will the insectoids rule some day? Brooks is cautious about making claims about the future of subsumption architecture, but he plans to push the idea to its limits. Will we find that as we add ever more complex layers of behavior that the subsumption approach will continue to work?

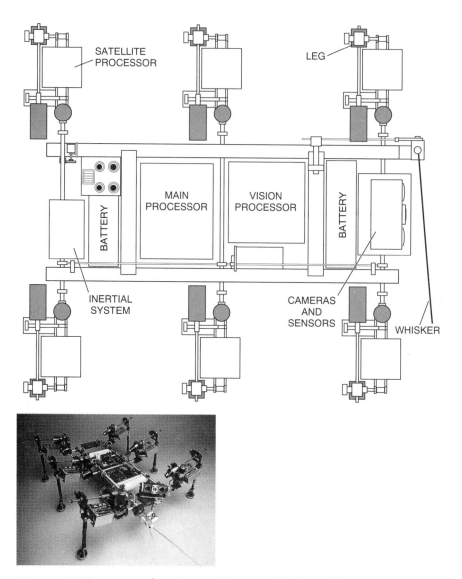

Figure 4.3 Anatomy of an insectoid named Attila is shown above and at left.

Or will we encounter a barrier that forces us to resort to something like traditional techniques? I am sure these questions will bug him for the foreseeable future.

Further Reading

Ivan Amato. "Gearing Down." *Science News*, Vol. 139, no. 2 (January 12, 1991), pp. 26–27.

A. K. Dewdney. "Braitenberg Memoirs: Vehicles for Probing Behavior Roam a Dark Plain Marked by Lights." *Scientific American* Computer Recreations, March 1987.

A. K. Dewdney. *The Magic Machine: A Handbook of Computer Sorcery.* W. H. Freeman, 1990.

Michael C. Smit and Mark W. Tilden. "Beam Robotics." *Algorithm*, Vol. 2, No. 2 (March 1991), pp. 15–19.

5

BUILDING A BRAIN

In man's brain the impressions from outside are . . .
the imprint of the external world . . .

VICTOR WEISSKOPF, *Knowledge and Wonder*

Neural networks, assemblies of artificial neurons that seem capable of learning an enormous variety of different tasks, have captured the imagination of researchers in recent years. But they have also intrigued recreational programmers to the point of despair. Where were the neural net programs you could write and run on a personal computer?

One now exists. Developed by Edward A. Rietman and Robert C. Frye of AT&T Bell Laboratories at Murray Hill, N. J. in the late 1980s, the program I call POLARNET converts polar coordinates to cartesian coordinates by trial and error. More than this, POLARNET learns the art of conversion by training on actual coordinates. The underlying algorithm is reasonably simple and the network's learning process is fascinating to watch. I have altered the algorithm slightly to make it easier for readers to program.

Special, parallel hardware demonstrates the parallel prowess of neurons best. But even an old-fashioned serial computer can simulate a neural net with reasonable electronic elan — if there are not too many neurons. The Rietman-Frye network requires only 30 to 40 neurons to learn coordinate conversions. A modern microcomputer can simulate a single wave of computation through as many neurons with no noticeable delay.

All learning networks share the same basic architecture shown in Figure 5.1. Information enters the network on the left through a layer of input neurons. It then passes through one or more layers of medial neurons and departs, on the right, through a layer of special output

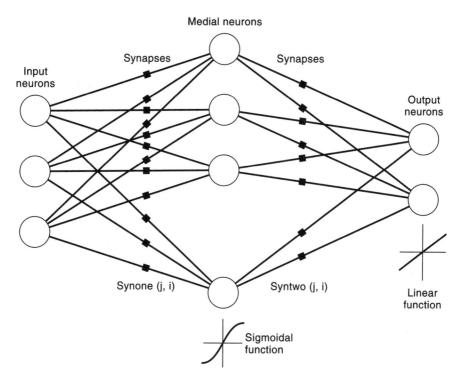

Figure 5.1 Generic mural network.

neurons. (The illustration, which applies to the Rietman-Frye network specifically, has only one medial layer.) The network processes the information as it flows through successive layers, from input to output. Each neuron in a given layer communicates with every neuron in the next layer via special synaptic connections. In formal terms, a synapse amounts to a multiplier, or weight, which modifies the number that is transmitted from one neuron to the other.

Individual neurons operate, like their biological counterparts, by a process of summation. Each neuron adds together all the signals that it receives. If it happens to reside in one of the medial layers, it will modify the sum of its signals further by applying a special, sigmoidal function that squeezes it non-linearly into the interval from −1 to +1: The larger a sum is, the more closely it will approach +1 or −1, depending on its sign. Figure 5.1 displays the general shape of a sigmoidal function just below the layer of medial neurons.

Sigmoidal functions enable neural networks to respond non-linearly to their environments. A great variety of actual functions, with names like the hyperbolic tangent, arc tangent, Fermi function, and so on, play the role quite nicely. Their ability to keep the outputs of intermediate neurons bounded (between 0 and 1) is just as important as their non-linear response. My version of POLARNET will use the Fermi function for this purpose:

$$1/(1 - e^{-x})$$

When the network embodied in POLARNET has been trained and is ready to run, the user of the program merely types in the polar coordinates to be converted. The program then gives the numbers to the two input neurons and the network does the rest, in a manner of speaking. With one layer of 30 medial neurons, for example, the input signals would automatically divide into 60 separate signals, 30 from each of the two input neurons to the medial neurons, via their synaptic connections. The medial neurons would then add together the two signals that each receives, apply its sigmoidal function, then send the signal to both output neurons through other synaptic connections. The output neurons simply add up the signals they receive. These are the two cartesian coordinates desired.

Some readers may be puzzled by the appearance in Figure 5.1 of three input neurons instead of two. The third neuron contains no coordinate information but provides, instead, a constant value that intermediate neurons may add to their other two inputs. The extra number gives the network an additional degree of freedom to shift signals by a constant or to avoid the unpleasant effects of zero inputs.

How do you educate a neural net? By giving it a lot of examples.

In truth, it is not the neurons that you educate, but the synaptic connections between them. Two arrays, called *synone* and *syntwo*, contain all the synaptic weights. The first array consists of the synapses between the input neurons and the medial ones. The second array consists of the second layer of synapses, those connecting the medial neurons to the output neurons. The net "learns" when it changes the synaptic weights in these arrays as a result of its experience with the coordinate pairs that it encounters.

Suppose that one of the training examples involves the conversion of the polar coordinates (15.7, 110°) to their cartesian equivalents,

(−5.37, 14.75). Normally, one would apply the standard sine and cosine formulas to transform the first set of coordinates into the second. But the network will split, multiply, sum, and manipulate the coordinates, recombining all the numbers at the output end. If the result does not match the desired cartesian coordinates, the network measures the error in each.

For example, if the neural network produces (−2.41, 10.82) instead of (−5.37, 14.75), it will develop two error differences, *e1* and *e2*, between the target coordinates and the computed ones: The individual differences, −2.96 and +3.93, form the basis for adjustments in the synaptic weights all the way through the net, from back to front. The method is called back-propagation.

In the Rietman-Frye network, the method first calculates how the weights in the second set of synapses must be changed to reduce the error if the same conversion were to be attempted again. To adjust the synaptic connection between the ith medial neuron and the jth output neuron, for example, POLARNET changes *syntwo(i, j)* by adding to it the product of the jth error and the previous output of the ith medial neuron. Thus, if the jth error is 3.93 and the previous output of the ith medial neuron was 8.82, the back-propagation method will add the product

$$3.93*8.82 = 34.66$$

to the value of *syntwo(i, j)*, revising it upward by this amount. If the same coordinate pair were re-submitted to the network revised only in this one synapse, the new contribution by the synapse to the final sum for the jth neuron would be 34.66 higher than it was before. If the earlier sum was 10.82, it would now become 45.48, considerably higher, even, than the target sum of 14.75.

To avoid problems of overshoot, an additional multiplier must enter the adjustment formula. A parameter called *rate*, usually with a value somewhere in the neighborhood of 0.1, modifies the adjustment to a kinder and gentler level, say 3.47. Thus, the new value of the jth output neuron would, in the case of this single adjustment, come to 14.29, very close (accidentally) to the target value.

Back propagation next alters the values of the first set of weights, contained in the array *synone*, by essentially the same method. First, however, the derivative of the sigmoid function must be applied to the back-propagated sum of the adjusted synapse values in *syntwo*. This step ensures that the error information goes through the same step in reverse that the processed information does in forward gear.

For each medial neuron, the back-propagation procedure forms the product between each of the two error terms and their corresponding synapse values for that particular medial neuron. It adds the two products together and then, pretending that this was the output of the medial neuron in question, computes the corresponding input error by using the derivative of the sigmoidal function, in this case, $y(1-y)$, where y is the signal to be back-propagated.

The weights stored in *synone* can now be changed in the final phase of back propagation. The actual adjustment, called *delta*, is the product of four numbers: The *rate* as described earlier, the reconstructed output as described in the paragraph above, the inverted form of this output, and the input to the neuron at the front end of the synaptic connection. The actual formula appears in Figure 5.2.

```
adjusting the second synaptic layer

for i ← 1 to 2
    for j ← 1 to n
        syntwo(j, i) ← syntwo(j, i) + rate*medout(j)*error(i)

inverting the sigmoidal signal

for i ← 1 to n
    sigma(i) ← 0
    for j ← 1 to 2
        sigma(i) ← sigma(i) + error(j)*syntwo(i, j)
    sigmoid(i) ← medin(i)*(1-medin(i)) / add error check

adjusting the first synaptic layer

for i ← 1 to 2
    for j ← 1 to n
        delta ← rate*sigmoid(j)*sigma(j)*input(i)
        synone(i, j) ← synone(i, j) + delta
```

Figure 5.2 Back-propagation algorithm.

Of course, one cycle of synapse changes does not automatically make the neural network a perfect coordinate converter. But many such changes will cause a slow and steady improvement.

The standard error, E, combines the two individual error terms (the square root of the sum of the squares of $e1$ and $e2$) to measure the network's accuracy at any given time. Figure 5.3 shows how E changed in an automated experiment involving 50,000 randomly selected coordinate conversion examples, each involving a point within one unit distance of the origin.

The network had 40 medial neurons and a rather modest learning *rate* of 0.01. The learning curve, in spite of frequent fluctuations, shows a determined downward trend from 25 percent down to about 4 percent. It reaches this level of competence shortly after 30,000 trials and does not improve much thereafter.

Networks with two medial layers may do better. For example, Rietman and Frye tested a network having two medial layers of 15 neurons

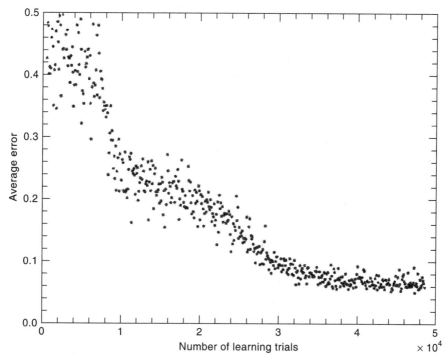

Figure 5.3 Learning curve of the polar converter.

each. When they tested this network on 50,000 conversion examples, it converged to a competence level of only 1.5 percent error, even by the 25,000th test.

Strangely enough, in the world of neural nets, bigger is not necessarily better. When Rietman and Frye increased the number of neurons in each medial layer from 15 to 150, the network barely managed a 2 percent error rate!

The foregoing description of the conversion network is just complete enough that readers with a modicum of programming experience will be able to write POLARNET without the benefit of further advice. To confirm one detail or another, they only need to consult the two algorithm boxes (Figures 5.2 and 5.4). Others will want to know what the symbols and variables in these algorithms mean. As usual, the for-loop stands for the standard iteration loop of which every programming language has some version. The left-pointing arrow means the assignment statement indicated by a " $=$ " or ":=" in most languages.

The algorithm in Figure 5.4 represents the normal operation of POLARNET. Before the program is run on a single example, however, all the synapses must be initialized by setting them to a random number between 0 and 0.1.

The first double for-loop achieves this by running through all possible combinations of one of the n medial neurons with one of the 3 input neurons. For each combination, it sets the corresponding value of *synone* to the product of 0.1 and a random number. Most computer systems produce random numbers between 0 and 1, so the product of such a random number with 0.1 will be a random number that is only one-tenth as large. The second double for-loop does essentially the same thing for the array *syntwo*.

Such small and variable values for the synapse weights are crucial to getting the network running. If the weights were all the same to begin with, they would stay the same throughout training and the network would never change its behavior in a meaningful way. Variety is the spice of learning.

"Normal operation" refers to the next two double for-loops. The wave of computation passes through neural nets of this general type one layer at a time. The first double loop calculates inputs to the medial layer by adding up the inputs *medin* to each, as weighted by the entries in *synone*. The second double loop does the same thing for the output neurons, adding up the weighted *medout* outputs. At the end of the second double loop, POLARNET computes the target values for the cartesian coordi-

```
initial synapse settings

for i ← 1 to n                          / n: number of medial neurons
    for j ← 1 to 3                      / 3: number of input neurons
        synone(j, i) ← 0.1*random

for i ← 1 to 2                          / 2: number of output neurons
    for j ← 1 to n
        syntwo(j, i ← 0.1*random

coordinate conversion

input input(1), input(2)
for i ← 1 to n
    medin(i) ← 0                        / medial input
    for j ← 1 to 3
        (medin(i) ← medin(i) + synone(j, i)*input(j)
    medout(i) ← 1/(1-exp(-medin(i)))  / add error check

for i ← 1 to 2
    output(i) ← 0
    for j ← 1 to n
        output(i) ← output(i) + syntwo(j, i)*medout(j)
    compute target(i)                   / using input(1) and input(2)
    error(i) ← target(i) − output(i)
```

Figure 5.4 Normal operation.

nates by using the standard sine and cosine formulas mentioned earlier. Readers may easily expand this macro-step into the appropriate code. Thus, *target(1)* is the cartesian x-coordinate and *target(2)* is the cartesian y-coordinate of the point the user inputs at the head of the conversion procedure. The two error terms, *error(1)* and *error(2)*, play a crucial role in the next procedure.

The algorithm in Figure 5.2 is the back-propagation algorithm as explained earlier in the paragraph on educating the synapses. The explanation is already complete enough that readers who compare each section of the algorithm with the corresponding description should have no difficulty producing working code. But programmers are hereby warned of a special problem that may occur when POLARNET computes the sigmoidal function during forward propagation or its derivative during back propagation. Extremely small or extremely large numbers can produce overflow errors. Specifically, during forward propagation, the program must test *medin(i)* to ensure that exponentiation does not exceed the available precision. It must also check that the denominator of the sigmoidal expression is not so close to zero that division will also cause overflow. The latter test must also be made during back propagation when the derivative of the sigmoidal function is being generated.

A version of POLARNET that simply sets up initial synaptic weights, performs one wave of computation, then one wave of back propagation, would be of little use. But if the blocks following the initialization steps are placed inside a loop, readers may enjoy the privilege of typing in pair after pair of co-ordinates, watching as the network becomes more and more accurate.

Unfortunately, it takes thousands of pairs of polar coordinates to train the net adequately. For this reason, the same loop should be made automatic according to the following little recipe in which all steps but the second refer to blocks within the two main algorithms:

```
initialization
for cnt <—1 to 10,000
    select random point
    convert coordinates
    back propagation
    output error E
```

To generate random points (r, a) from within the unit circle, first generate a standard random number (between 0 and 1) for the radius r. Then generate a second random number and convert it to an angle a, multiplying by 360 (for degrees) or 2π (for radians). The resulting points will not be uniformly distributed in the unit circle, but will tend to cluster around the origin. This bias will not harm the experiment but purists may want to remove it by applying a correction function to the first coordinate, r.

Outputting the error E could mean anything from printing the value to plotting it on the screen. A plot of error values such as those in the learning curve in Figure 5.3 not only makes the program more informative and absorbing to watch, it becomes an indispensible tool for monitoring the progress of the network in many experimental situations.

Rietman and Frye have developed an important visualization tool that some readers might wish to emulate. At each stage in the learning process, one can stop the experiments and examine visually how well the network, as currently configured, performs conversions. Why not convert the whole unit circle at once, then plot the result? If the polar grid of rays and concentric circles survives the conversion more or less intact, the network is performing well. But if the grid comes out squashed or distorted in some way, the network's education will not be complete.

Readers may alter POLARNET to taste. Not only may they change the total number of experiments (from 10,000, above), but they are also free to change the number of input neurons (3), output neurons (2) or medial neurons (n) to any number they like. They may even install two or more medial layers to see how much difference they make to the speed of learning. In such a case, however, both the forward compution and backward propagation procedures will be in for something of an overhaul.

The ability to alter the basic size and shape of the network raises a number of interesting questions that readers might like to investigate: First, how does the size of the *rate* parameter affect the network's learning ability? With higher and higher values of *rate*, learning may converge more quickly but speed has it risks: learning may suddenly diverge wildly! Another interesting question concerns the effect of the initial synaptic weights on the network's ability to learn quickly. Are there some choices for initial synaptic values that throw the neurons off-track? Or ones that bring the network up to speed sooner? The question is worth asking because neural nets usually amount to what computer scientists call hill-climbing routines. The initial direction specified by the first synaptic values will determine how fast the network finds the optimum value (or hill).

How much does a second layer of medial neurons improve performance of the learning network? A third layer? Do diminishing returns eventually set in?

What effect does the choice of training examples have on the network's performance? Perhaps, as a practical matter, it would be best to have specific training sets of coordinate pairs that would bring the network up to its optimum performance levels after only a few hundred trials, not many thousand! Grid points might work very well.

Although it cannot be guaranteed that neural netwoks will converge to useful behavior in every potential application, many problems have yet to be investigated in this respect. Suddenly, recreational computing looks more and more like original research. Here is one suggestion.

Can neural nets learn to do arithmetic? Using exactly the same architecture as the coordinate conversion network, readers can investigate the ultimate competence of networks at addition and multiplication. In both cases, the networks will have two inputs as before, but they will have only one output. The only other modification involves one small part of the program POLARNET: The error terms will involve the difference between the real sum (or product) and the one computed by the net. Does the network learn addition more quickly than multiplication? How accurate does it ever get at either task?

Neural networks have found a small niche in our software toolkit. How much larger that niche becomes will depend, ultimately, on the range of tasks that they can reliably learn to perform.

One can be mildly pessimistic that layered networks will find applications in any but the simplest problems. If the solution space has more than one local optimum (hill) for example, the network may well go rushing up the wrong optimum. But if it's just a question of time, parallel computers with neural elements will make solvable problems increasingly practical. In the meantime, thanks to Rietman and Frye, readers find themselves once again at the forefront — ready to tackle the latest computational paradigm for themselves.

Further Reading

E. A. Rietman. *Explorations in Parallel Processing.* Tab Books, 1990.

D. E. Rumelhart and J. L. McClelland, eds. *Parallel Processing: Explorations in the Microstructure of Cognition*, Vol. 1. MIT Press, 1986.

6
DANCE OF THE TUR-MITES

(Termites) . . . forge the complexion of a landscape
like no other organism except man.

WALTER LINSENMAIER, *Insects of the World*

Anyone who has ever seen a termite mound must have been impressed by the complex patterns of tunnels built by the industrious but mindless insects. Paradoxically, artificial forms of life that make termites look like geniuses in other departments can produce equally astounding creations. Take tur-mites, for example. They are squarish, cybernetic creatures that have the most rudimentary of brains. And yet as they move about on the infinite plane on which they live, they trace out strange patterns that appear to reflect an underlying intelligent design.

The tur-mites were inspired in part by Greg Turk while a graduate student at the University of North Carolina at Chapel Hill. In 1988 Turk first experimented with a special type of Turing machine, a basic model of computation. A Turing machine is usually assumed to operate on an infinite linear tape that is divided into cells. Turk, however, studied Turking machines that operate on a kind of two-dimensional tape — essentially the same plane on which the tur-mites roam. Converting a two-dimensional Turing machine into a tur-mite is simple and painless: abstract rules are replaced straightforwardly by a neural network. Such a conversion highlights an important theme in the theory of computation: one computational scheme often turns out to be equivalent to another, seemingly unrelated, one.

Turing machines are named after the British mathematician Alan M. Turing, who first proposed them as a way to define computation. In effect, a Turing machine is the ultimate digital computing machine. It can compute anything that a modern computer can — as long as it is given enough time.

One can visualize a Turing machine as it is shown in Figure 6.1: a black box equipped with a device that reads a symbol in a single cell of an infinitely long tape, writes a new symbol in the cell and moves the tape either forward or backward in order to examine the symbol in an adjacent cell. What is inside the black box? It does not really matter, as long as the box adheres strictly to a given table that lists what the Turing machine must do for every symbol read and for every one of the machine's possible "states." These may change with each cycle of operation. A cycle consists of the following three steps:

1. Read the symbol currently under the read/write device.
2. Look up the table entry given by the machine's current state and the symbol just read.
3. Write the symbol given by the table entry, move the tape in the direction indicated and enter the state shown.

Each table entry therefore has three parts: a symbol to be written on the current cell, a direction in which to move the tape and a state to enter.

To a Turing machine the tape's motion is relative. One could just as easily arrange for the tape to remain fixed and the machine to move itself from cell to cell. In fact, once one contemplates the idea of moving the

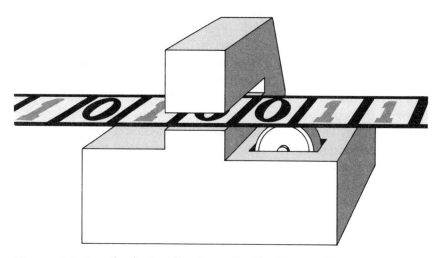

Figure 6.1 Standard visualization of a Turing machine.

Turing machine and not its tape, it does not take much imagination to envision a two-dimensional "tape" on which the machine may move about freely in not one but two independent directions.

Regardless of whether it has a one- or two-dimensional tape, a Turing machine's table is what ultimately determines its behavior. It is closely analogous to the program that controls a modern digital computer. In terms of computational capability, two-dimensional Turing machines are not more powerful than one-dimensional ones. They just have more interesting patterns of movement over the cells. The pattern shown in Figure 6.2, for example, was made by a single-state two-dimensional Turing machine. Its internal table is:

	BLACK	RED
A	(RED, LEFT, *A*)	(BLACK, RIGHT, *A*)

The machine's single state has been labeled *A*.

A slightly more complicated two-dimensional Turing machine that was discovered by Turk has two states, designated *A* and *B*, and it follows this internal table:

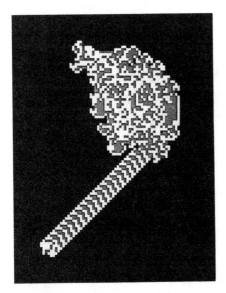

Figure 6.2 One of Turk's patterns.

	BLACK	GREEN
A	(GREEN, LEFT, *A*)	(BLACK FORWARD, *B*)
B	(GREEN, RIGHT, *A*)	(GREEN, RIGHT, *A*)

According to Turk, a two-dimensional Turing machine programmed with this table produces a marvelous spiral pattern. The machine creates "larger and larger patterned regions that are placed in orderly fashion around the starting point."

Any pattern generated by a two-dimensional Turing machine can be reproduced exactly by a tur-mite. A tur-mite's behavior, however, is not controlled by a mysterious black box. It is controlled by what can be loosely described as a brain. The fact that one can dissect and examine a tur-mite brain is what makes the creature so fascinating.

Judged only by its appearance and ethology, a tur-mite certainly is not fascinating (see Figure 6.3). Its body is roughly square, so that it fits snugly into the squares that divide the infinite plane on which it lives. It has a flat bottom equipped with some form of locomotory apparatus. (I

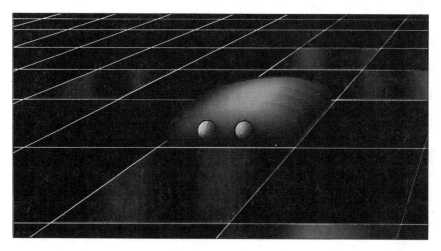

Figure 6.3 A tur-mite occupies one square at a time.

do not know what makes a tur-mite go, since I have never turned one over.) The apparatus enables the creature to rotate and to move exactly one square in the direction in which it happens to be facing. Actually, a turmite's face has no purpose except to let us know which way is forward; its "eyes" do not function. When a tur-mite changes direction, it merely swivels 90 degrees on its current square before moving to a new one.

Initially all the squares on the plane, including the one the tur-mite occupies, are black. Before it moves, however, a tur-mite may change the color of the square it currently occupies. (The tur-mite's color-changing organ is as mysterious as its locomotory apparatus.) A tur-mite that duplicates the pattern shown in Figure 6.2, for example, must be capable of painting the square one of two colors (in this case, red or black). To produce the pattern shown in Figure 6.4, however, a tur-mite has to have more colors at its disposal.

How does a tur-mite know when to move or when to change the color of its square? Those actions are controlled by its brain, which consists of a collection of "neurodes," simplified versions of the neurons in our own brain. A neurode receives signals along fibers that originate at sensors (which are found on a tur-mite's underside) or at other neurodes and sends signals along fibers to effectors (such as the tur-mite's locomotory apparatus or its color-changing organ) or to other neurodes.

A neurode fires (sends a signal along its output fiber) if the number of incoming signals equals or exceeds the neurode's threshold, which is given by the number written on the neurode. Otherwise, it does not fire. Because time in the tur-mite's world proceeds in discrete steps, all excitatory and inhibitory signals are sent or received in discrete steps as well.

To illustrate how a tur-mite actually makes a decision, I shall dissect the brain of two specimens (left and middle parts of Figure 6.5), both of which produce exactly the same pattern as that generated by the single-state two-dimensional Turing machine described earlier. The brain on the left contains two neurodes that are not connected to each other. Each neurode has just one input fiber and one output fiber. When the turmite's color sensor detects red, it sends a single signal to the left neurode, causing the neurode to fire. The neurode's output fiber splits into two parts, one going to the color effector (which then colors the entire square) and the other going to the locomotory apparatus (which then swivels the creature 90 degrees to the right and advances it one square in the new direction). On the other hand, when the tur-mite's color sensor detects black, it sends a signal to the right neurode, causing it to fire. The

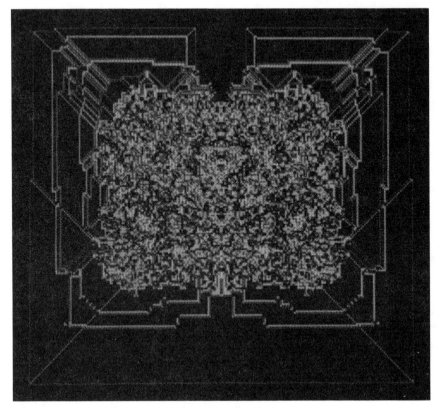

Figure 6.4 Multicolored tur-mite pattern.

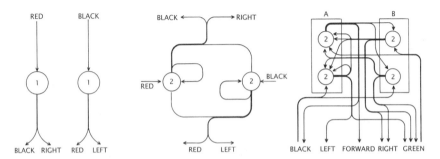

Figure 6.5 Three tur-mite brains, two of which (*left* and *center*) do the same job.

neurode's output, in turn, causes the tur-mite to paint the square red before turning and heading to the square on its left.

In short, when the tur-mite finds itself on a red square, it colors the square black and then moves one square to the right. And when the tur-mite occupies a black square, it changes the color of the square to red, then turns left and advances one square in its new direction.

The second tur-mite brain is more complicated, but it does exactly the same job as the first. It was derived by a method I shall presently describe. The two neurodes both have threshold 2; neither will fire unless it receives two input signals during the same time increment. Once the brain is set in motion, one neurode will always fire at each step in time.

The simple behavior embodied in the two neurode circuits just described results in the complicated image in Figure 6.2: a red cloud of tiny squares from which an intricate structure extends straight to infinity. What causes that sudden sense of purpose in the tur-mite after what seems a great deal of pointless meandering? The answer has to do with the pattern of colored squares in the cloud. At a certain point, part of that pattern, in combination with the tur-mite's neurode-based rules, locks the creature into a repetitive sequence of moves that weaves the structure. (I wonder if any readers can discover the triggering pattern.)

Life is like that for tur-mites. Sometimes a seemingly random meandering turns into an almost deadly determinism. Of course, the appearance of randomness is purely illusory. All tur-mites are decidedly deterministic at all times.

Nonetheless, there are mysteries to be found in the tur-mite's world. Consider, for example, the pattern shown in Figure 6.4. The tur-mite that made that pattern is outfitted with four effectors that change the color of a square to black, red, yellow or green. It abides by the following rules:

Square color	Action
black	paint red, turn right
red	paint yellow, turn right
yellow	paint green, turn left
green	paint black, turn left

This tur-mite also has a very simple brain. It consists of four neurodes that are not interconnected. Each neurode executes one of the four behavioral rules in the manner of the first tur-mite's simplest brain. Turk is puzzled by the fact that this particular tur-mite produces a pattern having bilateral symmetry. Readers can explore different versions of this machine in which the move sequence (right, right, left, left) is rotated to (right, left, left, right) and beyond.

How exactly does one get a tur-mite from a particular two-dimensional Turing machine? The technique is actually quite simple. One merely replaces each entry of the machine's internal table with a threshold-2 neurode that receives input signals from a sensor for the color corresponding to the entry's column and perhaps from other neurodes as well. Each neurode's output fibers go to the effectors necessary to execute the moves and color changes listed in the table entry.

For example, suppose that a certain neurode corresponds to a table entry in a column labeled "red" and a row labeled "*B*." According to the conversion scheme, the neurode would have an input fiber from the sensor that detects red. If the table entry happened to be (black, left, *B*), then the neurode would send an output fiber to the effector that colors the occupied square black and to the effector that enables the tur-mite to execute left turns.

The various states of a particular Turing machine are realized by the connections between neurodes in a tur-mite brain. Because the table entry in the example requires the tur-mite to adopt state *B*, the neurode representing that entry would extend output fibers to each of the neurodes making up row *B* of the table.

In this context, such a neural network is nothing more (and nothing less) than a form of hardware embodying a behavioral table. A sample conversion is displayed schematically in the right-hand part of Figure 6.5. It shows how one would go about constructing the brain of the tur-mite that mimics the behavior of Turk's spiraling two-dimensional Turking machine.

It is fun to watch a tur-mite (or a two-dimensional Turing machine) wander about on a cellular plane. To follow the action, however, the reader must write a program that simulates the tur-mite's movements. How does one go from a table to a program?

Luckily, the process is nearly as simple as designing a tur-mite's brain. A program that I call TURMITE consults a Turing-machine table in the form of three separate arrays: *color, motion* and *state*. Each array is indexed by two variables, *c* and *s*. The variable *c* indexes the color of the present square, and the variable *s* indexes the Turing machine's (or the equivalent tur-mite's) current state. Because the indexes have to be assigned integer values, the colors and states used in the simulation must be numbered.

For example, the colors black and green can be assigned to the variable c by the numbers 1 and 2, respectively. Similarly, the states A and B can be designated respectively by the values 1 and 2 of the variable s. In this case, a simulation of a spiraling tur-mite would require the following arrays:

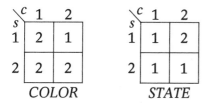

c	1	2
s		
1	2	1
2	2	2

COLOR

c	1	2
s		
1	1	2
2	1	1

STATE

Directions of motion must also be coded in terms of numbers. Hence, forward, backward, left and right could be indicated respectively by the numbers 1, 2, 3 and 4, which are contained in the array *motion*.

The main purpose of TURMITE is to color small squares (perhaps individual pixels) on the computer's display screen that highlight a turmite's peripatetics. The program keeps track of the displayed squares' colors in a two-dimensional array called *pattern*. Initially only one square is lit—the one lying at the center of the screen.

The value of c at any given time is provided by the entry in the array *pattern* corresponding to the turmite's current coordinates on the screen, say i and j. With c and s in hand, the program simply looks up the array entries *color(c,s)*, *motion(c,s)* and *state(c,s)*.

The program changes the color encoded in the entry in *pattern(i,j)* and then alters either i or j, depending on the value of *motion(c,s)*. Here the program must translate the relative movement encoded in *motion* into an absolute movement by consulting another variable, *dir*, which contains the last direction moved: up, down, left or right. The final step in TURMITE's operating cycle consists merely of changing s to the number given by *state(c,s)*. The rest can be left to the imagination and inventive skill of those readers who like to write their own programs.

Readers might even want to continue a new investigation begun by Norwegian computer scientist Odd Arild Olsen. Since Turk's initial turmite experiments in 1988, the creatures have enjoyed a certain endemic popularity with programmers who treasure behavioral exotica, not to mention those who probe the relationship between computation and "behavior," broadly defined. Olsen, who places not one but two turmites on the plane at a time, reports amazing relationships developed by

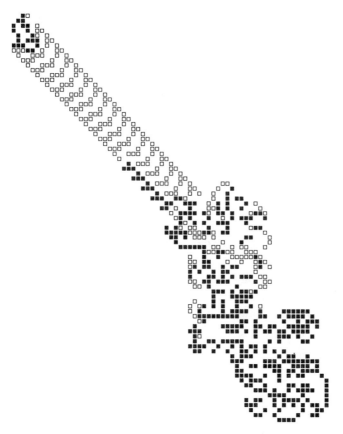

Figure 6.6 Two tur-mites build a nest and a burrow.

the pair. In particular he has systematically explored the behavior of the one-state tur-mite (described at the beginning of this chapter) when paired with itself.

The screen shown in Figure 6.6 captures just one of 1,681 behaviors Olsen has examined. In this case the tur-mites "cooperated" to build a "nest." Then one of them, perhaps growing restless, built a complicated burrow, seemingly toward infinity. The second tur-mite found the burrow, followed it to the end, and forced the first tur-mite to follow the burrow back to the nest. The second tur-mite also worked its way back, slowly recoloring all the squares! The 1,681 experiments performed by Olsen amounted to nothing more complicated than placing the first tur-mite at the origin of the grid, then placing the second tur-mite at one of the 1,681 grid locations with x- and y-coordinates ranging from -20 to $+20$. In all experiments, both tur-mites began with the same orientation. Olsen suggests that readers might explore what happens when tur-mites of *different* species are put on the plane.

Whether one is constructing a tur-mite's brain or simulating its behavior on a computer, it is interesting to reflect on the fact that, since tur-mites can carry out any computation a Turing machine is capable of executing, tur-mites can be just as powerful as some computers. If, as some claim, the human brain amounts to nothing more than a kind of digital computer, then some tur-mites could be just as smart as we are — if not smarter!

Further Reading

Martin Gardner. "Mathematical Games." *Scientific American,* Vol. 216, No. 3 (March 1967), pp. 124–129.
Martin Gardner. "Mathematical Games." *Scientific American,* Vol. 229, No. 5 (November 1973), pp. 116–123.

THEME TWO

MATTER MISBEHAVES

To say that matter misbehaves may serve to
catch the reader's eye but it does a disservice
to matter itself. Matter does not break its own
laws the way humans break theirs. Since the
arrival of computers, we have learned to
program the laws we know and to simulate
the behavior of matter in many of its
manifestations.

The science of simulation enables us to
predict weather (up to a point), to design new
structures, and to probe the details of
molecular interactions, all without recourse to
the laboratory. But the magic of this science
has been pulled up short by the discovery that
some physical systems will evade the power of
any computer to predict. Chaos has arrived.

The theme opens mildly enough with two
computer games, each of them involving a
dynamical system. A golf ball, gently tapped
by an abstract putter, rolls across the green
and narrowly misses the hole. A spaceship
changes its orbit around the sun when a
computer programmer types in a new thrust
factor. Here, students of the new science learn
how to turn Newtonian dynamics into
behavior on the screen. But chaos lurks in the
background already.

The next dynamical system, Lorenz's water
wheel, captures all the dynamics of his famous
weather-in-a-jar model, historically one of the
first models of chaos. It turns out that the
simplest weather system of all, air circulating

in a heated jar, exhibits the exquisite sensitivity to initial conditions that we call chaos. But it's easier to see buckets revolving chaotically on a water wheel than to spot invisible air in a jar. A peek at the system's attractor immediately reveals its fractal nature, the Lorenz attractor.

Lyapunov space maps the behavior of a choatic system. For every combination of parameter values that determine the system's behavior, the color of this space reflects whether chaos is present or absent. The ultra-simple logistic system gives rise to a space filled with strange, fractal swallows and fantastic fairy bridges over alien cities. The Lyapunov exponent not only enables probers of systems to detect chaos, it enables them to map all the possibilities at once.

One of the most notable advances in the science of fractals, the iterated function systems of Michael F. Barnsley, enable us to custom-design our own fractals, from infinite fern leaves to smoky clouds. The principles, spelled out as an innocent game of fractal tennis, become specific programming advice in the very next chapter.

The foregoing chapters develop the theme of misbehaving matter in that special order that clarifies the relationships among three key subjects. First come dynamical systems, then chaos, then fractals. Readers who understand dynamical systems will have an easier time appreciating what chaos really means. At the same time chaos itself has a shape. The real significance of fractals lies not in the happy shapes of puffy clouds but in the nightmarish forms that lurk in the "phase-space" of their dynamical systems. The first step in dealing effectively with chaos is to inspect it in the glaring light of the computer microscope.

MICRO-MINIATURE GOLF

I have once, it is true, had the distinction 'of making a
hole in one'. . . . That is to say, after I had hit, a ball
was found in the can, and my ball was not found. It is
what we call circumstantial evidence — the same
thing that people are hanged for.

STEVEN LEACOCK, "Mathematics for Golfers," in *The
World of Mathematics*, Volume 4

T he ordinary golfer deploying an armory of clubs tries desperately
to drive a small ball into a distant hole hidden in several acres of grass
and guarded by ponds, trees, and sand traps. Players of miniature golf
use but one club on a much smaller obstacle course of bumps, tunnels,
rotating blades and swinging pendulums. Now players of micro-miniature golf, without swinging a club at all, can attempt a hole in one on the
screen of a microcomputer. There are hazards here, too, including some
that violate the laws of physics.

Although the microgolfer is confined to an armchair, he or she can
putt with an electronic club and even enjoy a dimension not available to
players of the larger games: programming. How many of us are able to
design, build, and play a course all in the same day? Not even Jack
Nicklaus — unless he knows how to program. In fact Nicklaus would not
even have to be a professional programmer to set up a microgolf course.

I shall lay down plans for three holes: one for beginners and two for
more advanced players. At the end of the day everyone who plays by the
rules will have made a microgolf course on a par with his or her talents.

The project is illustrated in its simplest form in Figure 7.1. Here the
program I call HOLE IN ONE has displayed a single hole on a rectangular
green. A putter appears as a short line segment behind a tiny ball at one

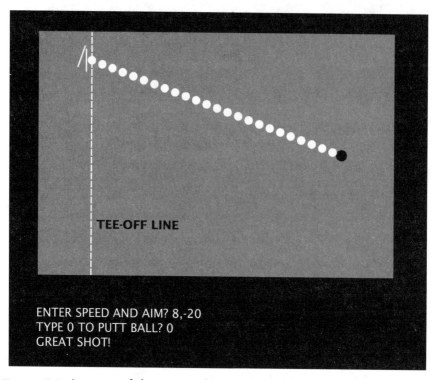

ENTER SPEED AND AIM? 8,-20
TYPE 0 TO PUTT BALL? 0
GREAT SHOT!

Figure 7.1 A successful putt on the HOLE IN ONE green.

end of the green. A player angles and positions the putter to aim and strike the ball toward its target, the cup at the other end of the green.

The simple HOLE IN ONE version of microgolf is all hit or miss. If the ball goes past the cup, it will cross over the course's edge as though it were not there, disappearing off the screen and rolling into the computer's memory, never to reappear. Even this version of the game has a certain pleasurable tension to it.

It is actually possible for an amateur to prepare HOLE IN ONE as a kind of software springboard to the more advanced versions. Fragments of the program HOLE IN ONE can be inserted into the programs I call BIRDIE and EAGLE, which are depicted in Figures 7.2 and 7.3, respectively.

BIRDIE features a hazard near the cup, a circular twilight zone of sorts. If the ball enters this zone, it changes direction and speed in a completely unpredictable manner. More treacherous hazards plague the EAGLE green, but I will withhold the horrifying details for now.

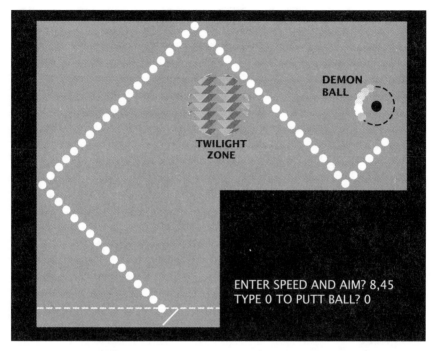

Figure 7.2 A twilight zone and a demon ball make life difficult for the intermediate putter.

In this chapter I have provided a more detailed program description for those hesitant or beginning programmers who need just a bit of extra information to get started. The following description of HOLE IN ONE adopts the tried-and-true method of starting with a clear description of the computation to be performed, usually given in steps as an algorithm. From there it moves, as fast as possible, to actual fragments of program. A reader who puts all the pieces together is just a few keystrokes away from the Micro-Miniature Open!

HOLE IN ONE first displays the cup ready for play, and then it requests that a player adjust the putter and putt. HOLE IN ONE then draws and redraws the ball as it rolls across the electronic turf, perhaps into the hole.

From these specifications a crude algorithm for HOLE IN ONE can be devised: draw the layout, prompt the user to putt, move the ball many times (to animate the direction and speed of the putt) and decide each time whether the ball has fallen into the cup. The algorithm can then be refined to create the program HOLE IN ONE. To begin with, the initial

Figure 7.3 Three hazards on the advanced green.

layout can be displayed in a few steps that draw the green, cup, ball, and putter. These steps can be programmed easily.

In order to be helpfully explicit, I shall assume that the reader is writing a program in the BASIC language on an IBM PC or a PC-compatible computer. (Do not be discouraged if you lack the hardware. The program is easily adapted to other computer systems.) To be even more explicit, I shall pretend that all readers have a screen at least 300 pixels (screen dots) wide and 200 pixels high. All distances on the screen must be measured from the origin, which is the top left corner of the IBM screen.

On a 300-by-200 pixel screen it is quite reasonable to draw a rectangular green 240 pixels long and 160 pixels high. To center the layout more or less on the screen, HOLE IN ONE places the green 30 pixels from the left side of the screen and 20 pixels from the top. In short, the horizontal coordinates of the green run from 30 to 270 and its vertical coordinates run from 20 to 180. The green takes shape from the following instructions:

```
10 SCREEN 1
20 LINE (30,20) — (270,20)
30 LINE (30,180) — (270,180)
40 LINE (30,20) — (30,180)
50 LINE (270,20) — (270,180)
```

Note that by numbering BASIC statements with increasing (but not necessarily consecutive) values, the programmer designates the exact order in which the computer should execute those statements. The first command, CLS, clears the screen of any images that may previously have been drawn on it. This feature is employed when one wishes to restart the program.

HOLE IN ONE next represents the cup as a circle at the far right end of the rectangle. The center of the cup is 240 pixels from the left and 100 pixels from the top. The BASIC instruction that will draw the cup is therefore

```
60 CIRCLE (240,100),5,1
```

The circle is centered on the coordinates (240,100) and has a radius of five pixels. The "1" at the end of the line specifies the color white.

Just to keep the shot from being boring, HOLE IN ONE places the ball at a random location along the tee-off line, which is 30 pixels from the left end of the green. Because the ball's position changes throughout the program, the variables *XBALL* and *YBALL* are created to keep track of its coordinates

```
70 XBALL = 60
80 YBALL = 160*RND + 20
90 CIRCLE (XBALL,YBALL),4,1
```

Line 70 restricts the ball's x coordinate to coincide with the tee-off line. Line 80 selects a random number between zero and one called RND, scales it up to the size of a number between zero and 160 and then adds 20 to the result. This means that *YBALL* will lie somewhere along the tee-off line. Line 90 draws the ball with its center at (*XBALL,YBALL*). The ball has a radius of four, a snug fit in the radius-five hole.

A line just behind the ball represents the putter, or more accurately the blade of the putter. Its resting state is given by the following:

100 LINE (54,YBALL + 8) − (54,YBALL − 8)

This vertical line is tangent to the left side of the ball and is 16 pixels long.

The next step of the HOLE IN ONE algorithm — to "prompt the user to putt" — must be refined just a little before programming continues. "To prompt" means not only to send a message that asks a player to putt but also to acquire information about the orientation of the putter and the speed of the swing. It also means that HOLE IN ONE must redraw the putter in its new position so that a player can judge the shot by eye.

Two lines of BASIC are added to HOLE IN ONE, both to print a message and to accept input.

110 PRINT "ENTER SPEED AND AIM"
120 INPUT SPEED, AIM

The variable called *SPEED* stores the distance in pixels that the ball moves every time HOLE IN ONE updates its position in the course of a putt.

The variable *AIM* stores the ball's direction of motion. Many players will find degrees to be the natural unit for entering an angle for *AIM*. HOLE IN ONE therefore accepts an angle between + 90 and − 90 degrees as measured from a horizontal line. The extremes represent strokes that send the ball straight up or down.

Unfortunately, most versions of BASIC handle angular measurements in units called radians rather than in degrees. Therefore, HOLE IN ONE requires a small calculation that converts degrees into radians.

130 *RADAIM* = (*AIM**3.1416)/180

The conversion is based on the fact that 180 degrees equals π radians.

The values of *RADAIM* and *SPEED* can be inserted into a formula that determines the position and orientation of the putter. HOLE IN ONE requires the formula to draw the putter poised either to stroke the ball into the cup or to whack it off the green.

The formula positions the center of the putter behind the ball along the stroke line and at a distance proportional to the value of SPEED. The putter should just touch the ball's surface when SPEED equals zero, that is, it should be at least three pixels to the left of the ball's center. The x coordinate of the putter's center is therefore discovered by subtracting (*SPEED* + 3) times the cosine of *RADAIM* from *XBALL*. The y coordinate will be found by adding (*SPEED* + 3) times the sine of *RADAIM* to *YBALL*.

To angle the putter, HOLE IN ONE requires a little more trigonometry. Since the putter is 16 pixels long, its end points are eight pixels away from the center. The displacement along the *x* axis is then eight times the cosine of *RADAIM*, and along the *y* axis it is eight times the sine of *RA-DAIM*.

These quantities, denoted by *A, B, C* and *D*, respectively, in the program fragment below, are all computed separately on lines 140 to 170. The actual coordinates of the putter's "top" end (*XTOP,YTOP*) and "bottom" end (*XBOT,YBOT*) are then computed. Finally, in line 220 the putter is drawn as a line connecting these points.

```
140 A = 8*COS (RADAIM)
150 B = 8*SIN (RADAIM)
160 C = (SPEED + 3)*COS (RADAIM)
170 D = (SPEED + 3)*SIN (RADAIM)
180 XTOP = XBALL − C + B
190 YTOP = YBALL + D + A
200 XBOT = XBALL − C − B
210 YBOT = YBALL + D − A
220 LINE (XTOP,YTOP) − (XBOT,YBOT)
```

It might appear at this point that the program is ready to enter the third phase of its operation, to produce the animation of the ball heading toward the cup. Has anything been left out? What if a player decides that the angle of the putter looks wrong. Surely the fallible human being should be given a second chance. This is done by branching back to line 10 at the player's option.

```
230 PRINT "TYPE 0 to PUTT BALL"
240 INPUT PUTT
250 IF PUTT < > 0 THEN GOTO 10
```

Here, if the player types any number but zero, the program will branch back to line 10, where it will clear the screen, redraw the green and prompt the player again for new values of *AIM* and *SPEED*. If the player types zero, HOLE IN ONE will proceed to the final phase of its operation, the one specified much earlier by the phrase "move the ball many times to animate the direction and speed of the putt."

To move the ball, however, HOLE IN ONE must increase the *x* and *y* coordinates of the ball independently. To this end, the variable *SPEED* is decomposed into two new variables, one called *XSPEED* in the *x* direction and one called *YSPEED* in the *y* direction.

```
260 XSPEED = SPEED*COS (RADAIM)
270 YSPEED = SPEED*SIN (RADAIM)
```

The final section of the program consists of a loop within which two operations will be performed continually. The ball will be moved and then checked to see whether it happens to be in the cup.

```
280 FOR K = 1 to 300
290 XBALL = XBALL + XSPEED
300 YBALL = YBALL + YSPEED
310 CIRCLE(XBALL,YBALL),4,1
320 IF ABS(XBALL − 240) > 4
    THEN GOTO 360
330 IF ABS(YBALL − 100) > 4
    THEN GOTO 360
340 XSPEED = 0
350 YSPEED = 0
360 NEXT K
```

The instruction on line 280 sets up the simplest kind of loop. A variable K counts from one to 300 to ensure enough move-and-draw cycles for the ball to make it to the cup even at a speed of one. Within the loop the new ball coordinates are updated, and at line 310 the ball is drawn.

Lines 320 and 330 test the ball's coordinates separately to find out whether the ball is in the cup. If it is not, the program skips down to line 360. If it is, the ball's two speed coordinates are reset to zero, effectively freezing the ball.

Professionals may object to this "for" loop because the program continues to run even when the ball drops into the cup. HOLE IN ONE tests the ball's coordinates until the count K reaches 300. To remedy this, the amateur golf programmer might add three instructions to the end of the program. One would test whether the speed of the ball is zero. If the test is affirmative, a second instruction could print a pat-on-the-back message such as "GREAT SHOT!" A final instruction, required by most versions of BASIC, marks the end of the program with the word "END."

This completes HOLE IN ONE. Readers who type in the program and run it will notice a peculiar effect as they try to putt the ball at different *SPEED*'s. The unusual discrete physics that appears to operate in the microgolf world of HOLE IN ONE will produce a hole in one only if the speed of the ball divides the distance to the cup evenly!

What might be considered a defect from one point of view may be regarded as a "feature" from another; if the physics is wild by accident, perhaps it can also be so by design. BIRDIE features some hazards not seen on any grass turf. In addition, the ball bounces around the green.

To describe these golfing wonders, I will shift expositional gears to exclude IBM PC's and BASIC, reverting to algorithmic language. The BIRDIE course shown in Figure 7.2 is L-shaped. How does BIRDIE ensure that the ball stays within the borders as it rolls? Even in the strange world of microgolf, the angle of reflection must equal the angle of incidence. This is not difficult to set up for the six segments of border, which may be called *wall1* through *wall6* without worrying too much about which wall is which. Each time the main display loop calculates a new position for the ball, BIRDIE will check to see whether any of the walls has been crossed. For example, if *wall1* has been crossed, BIRDIE should reflect the ball.

When the test and its (possibly) resulting reflection have been executed, the program checks *wall2* and then *wall3* and so on. An interesting problem surfaces at this point. What if the ball, in "striking" one wall and then receiving its subsequent reflection, now finds itself outside another wall? Is there not a possibility that if the ball is destined to hit a wall near a corner, it will bounce only from one wall but not from the other? Readers who ponder the point properly will develop a successful solution.

Once the ball has done all the rebounding it is destined to do in the current cycle, BIRDIE displays it and tests whether the ball is in the cup just as HOLE IN ONE does. What if the unlucky putter misses the cup? The ball will continue to bounce around within the confines of the green until it either enters the cup or falls into an endless cycle of rebounds. Some duffers will find this a wonderful proposition; others will sneer at the lack of realism. The game lacks that all-important factor, friction!

To allow the ball to be slowed to a stop, BIRDIE multiplies *SPEED* by some constant that is less than one, say .995, each time the program goes through its move-and-test loop. Because *SPEED* decreases by a factor of .995 each time through the loop, both *XSPEED* and *YSPEED* will also be multiplied by this constant within the loop.

It may of course happen that the ball eventually slows to zero without having dropped into the cup. In this case BIRDIE must call a halt to the loop, and so the loop must be not of the "for" type but of the "while" type. The second kind of loop keeps the cycle going as long as (while) some condition holds. In this case the condition is that *SPEED* be greater than some rather small number such as 0.5. At such a point BIRDIE sends the user back to the interactive part of the program where he or she is prompted for a putt.

What hazards does the hapless golfer encounter on the second hole? One hazard is referred to as a circular twilight zone. Having entered the zone, the ball suffers a random change in its current direction. What happens is that BIRDIE tests whether the ball lies within the charmed circle and, if it does, changes the angle *RADAIM* by a random number between -10 and $+10$. By planning a careful series of bounces, a good putter can send the ball around the twilight zone.

The second hazard is harder to avoid. A demon ball orbits the cup at a fixed distance. It completes an orbit for every 10 cycles of the loop. If the player's ball happens to touch the demon ball, the player's ball reappears back at the tee-off line. Most readers who have followed the course this far will probably think of a way to manage this awe-inspiring event.

EAGLE, as the elaborate illustration in Figure 7.3 shows, has a more complicated green than BIRDIE. Largely a glorified version of BIRDIE, it features some advanced hazards. For example, whenever the ball traverses the neck connecting one end of the layout to the other, it experiences a force pulling toward the neck's center. The force is related to the ball's distance from the centerline, as though the passage were gracefully banked. There is also a sand trap, where the *SPEED* is decreased not by a factor of .995 but by .9. Only the most careful of strokes will get one out of the trap without sending the ball careening around the layout like a runaway bullet. The final hazard involves a bit of "rough." Here the ball becomes lost, disappearing before it even rolls to a stop. How to find the ball? If you reposition the putter in the right location, the ball will appear beside it.

I was inspired to take readers on a tour of microgolf greenery by way of a game called Zany Golf, distributed by Electronic Arts in San Mateo, California. One can buy the game, of course, but that might mean missing the fun of building one's own. Readers are by no means limited to golf, in any case. The techniques described here lend themselves readily to games of micropinball and electronic billiards.

Further Reading

Bruce A. Artwick. *Microcomputer Displays, Graphics, and Animation*. Prentice Hall, 1984.

8

STAR TREK DYNAMICS

In the early 1970's I often worked late at my university office in the hope of avoiding the interruptions of students. Unfortunately, just down the corridor in the computer-graphics research laboratory was the nightly gathering for a favorite student game variously called Star Trek or Space War. "Get him! Get him!" came the cries that echoed through my closed office door. "Watch out for the missiles!" The noise was just enough to disrupt my train of thought. Unable to beat Star Trek, I would usually join it. With a resolve to return to less frivolous matters as soon as the stretch had refocused my attention, I would stroll down to the lab to watch the action.

The game Star Trek is loosely based on the television series of the same name; the competition is a battle between the starship *Enterprise* and a Klingon battle cruiser. Aficionados of the television program will recall that *Enterprise* traveled where human beings had never ventured before. The exploration was done on behalf of a collection of cooperating races called the Federation, which was apparently dominated by humans. Klingons were the hirsute rivals of the Federation for the domination of the Milky Way, if not of the entire universe.

Although Star Trek originally required a powerful graphics-research computer, it can now be programmed comfortably on a personal machine. The two starships orbit a central sun, launching missiles at each other and dodging the return fire. Both ships and missiles are subject to gravity, and orbital motion determines much of the action. Pilots without a reasonable feel for celestial mechanics incinerate their ships in the sun or unintentionally cross the deceptive trajectory of a missile's orbit. The side whose ship blows up first is the loser.

At one time versions of Star Trek had appeared at hundreds of universities and other institutions; the game was officially frowned on but secretly enjoyed. I find it ironic that years after those late-night interruptions I still recall the game with fondness. Star Trek was only one of the many games developed by students, and most such games soon found their way into commercial packages that were largely responsible for the revolution in home computers. Commercial versions of Star Trek have only recently been introduced, although arcade versions have been available for some time.

The version of Star Trek described here takes the reader back to the clandestine romance of the earliest computer games. Furthermore, it serves to introduce the arcane subject of arcade programming. One goal is to keep the screen alive: the computations that create the action in the Star Trek world must be as fast and as simple as possible. A second programming goal is to create a realistic gravitational environment, but here too readers have encountered the same problem in somewhat different guise. In *The Armchair Universe* I introduced a star cluster in which stars dance about in accordance with their mutual gravitational attraction. Gravity of a simpler kind warps the tracks of ships and missiles in Star Trek. Only the central sun exerts a perceptible force.

To engage in their orbital duel two players sit at the keyboard of a computer and press the keys assigned to control their ships. One player, perhaps the hairier one, takes command of the Klingon ship; the other guards the fortunes of the Federation. At first only the central sun and the two ships occupy the screen. The sun is a circle and the ships are icons with just enough detail for distinguishing friend from foe (see Figures 8.1 and 8.2).

When the game begins, both ships are in free fall toward the sun. The players immediately turn their ships away from the fall line and fire their rocket engines to bring the ships into safe orbit. A ship that touches the sun instantly vaporizes and of course the game is lost.

As soon as the orbits are established, each player begins trying to eliminate his opponent. One extreme tactic is to lie in wait until the enemy ship passes nearby. A quick salvo may then finish it off. Another extreme is trickier: one can try to aim the shots from a position on the opposite side of the sun. On the screen bright points of light—called photon torpedos on the television program—fly outward from the firing vessel and burn their way around the sun in a gently curving array of menace. Unless the enemy ship is commanded by a pilot of extraordinary skill, the ship is destined to meet one of the missiles and explode in a burst of interstellar debris. The screen signals the event with a brief cloud of dots and announces either VICTORY FOR THE FEDERATION or VICTORY FOR THE KLINGON FORCES.

Because the action near the sun is so intense, cautious players prefer to orbit farther out. The main disadvantage of the strategy is the need to recharge a solar energy cell. The control of each ship depends on its energy cell. When the cell is spent, the ship must quickly move closer to the sun to replenish its supply of solar photons. In a distant orbit the photon stream is weak and the ship runs the risk of becoming a sitting duck.

There is another tricky feature to be aware of in high orbital flight: the battle space in Star Trek is "toroidal." In other words, if the ship moves too close to one edge of the screen, it will disappear there and reappear near the opposite edge.

Each ship has an infinite supply of missiles, but there can never be more than 10 of them in flight at the same time. The missiles obey the same laws of physics as the ships do. A missile lasts either until it strikes a ship (including its own) or until it runs out of fuel. So much for the game.

The program I call TREK is the most ambitious one presented in this book, not so much because of its complexity as because of its length. Some of the more standard routines can only be sketched in. Programming neophytes may nonetheless try the project with some hope of success and considerable entertainment.

TREK cycles through six major sections of code as long as both ships are operational:

Read the keys.
Update ship and missile positions.
Check for contacts.
Update energy of ships.
Manage missiles.
Display.

With the possible exception of the first section, many readers will find that TREK is relatively straightforward to write. Reading keys will be

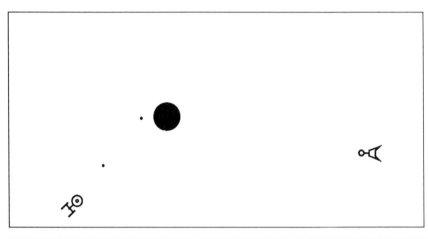

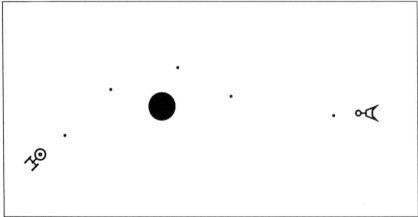

Figure 8.1 *Enterprise* and the Klingon battle cruiser exchange missiles.

new to some, but the facility is indispensable for arcade programming. Most high-level languages have statements that enable a program to test whether a particular key has been pressed.

For example, in the language Micro-soft BASIC the relevant command is

    On key(k) gosub n.

When the "On key" command is executed, the program checks at the beginning of every subsequent command to determine whether or not key k was pressed. If it was, the program branches to the command at

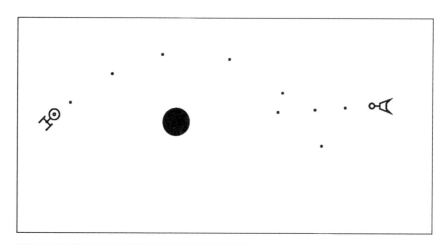

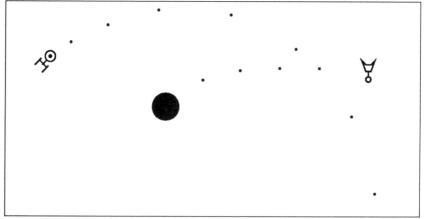

line *n*. At line *n* a subroutine begins whose purpose is to record the pressing of key *k*, generally by assigning some value to a "flag" variable. There are 14 specific keys on the keyboard of the IBM PC that can be checked in this way: the 10 function keys and the four cursor-control keys. One must assign four keys to each player — say function keys *F*1, *F*2, *F*3 and *F*4 to the Federation forces and the four cursor keys to the Klingon forces. The numbers for this assignment are respectively 1 through 4 and 11 through 14. A manual is indispensable here.

    For each side the first of the four keys controls thrust, the next two control direction and the last one controls the firing of missiles. The thrust key simply imparts a fixed thrust, at full throttle, for one program

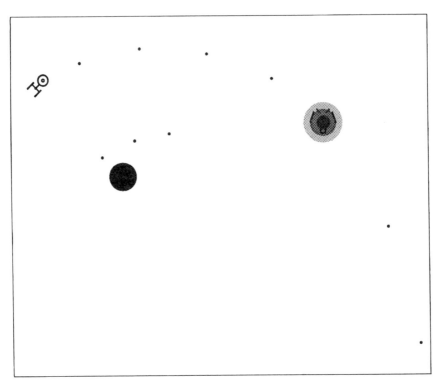

Figure 8.2 The Klingon ship is not able to dodge the barrage.

cycle. Each press of a direction key turns the corresponding starship through an angle of 10 degrees. A tap on the missile key fires a single missile. Before playing the game it is useful to stick small square labels on the controlling keys. Appropriate symbols marked on the labels can then remind the combatants which key does what.

The program TREK must include an "On key" command for each of the eight designated controlling keys. "On key" is not executed unless it is preceded by the command "Key(*k*) on."

All the subroutines to which TREK branches from "On key" commands are simple and essentially the same. Each subroutine is made up of two instructions. The first instruction sets a flag variable to 1 for later consultation by the program; the second causes a return of the program execution to the line number of the "On key" command that invoked the subroutine. The flag variables for the control of *Enterprise* might as well be called *fdgo, fdrt, fdlt* and *fdfr*. They stand for "Federation go" (turn on thruster), "Federation right" (turn clockwise), "Federation left" (turn counterclockwise) and "Federation fire" (shoot a missile). Similarly, the variables *kngo, knrt, knlt* and *knfr* record the thrust, direction and missile firing of the Klingon battle cruiser.

When a flag variable is set to 1 within a subroutine, it triggers a change in one of the starships. For example, when *fdgo* is 1, the position-updating segment of the program adds a small acceleration (between 2 and 5, according to taste) to the current acceleration of *Enterprise*. TREK must then reset the flag to 0.

Updating the positions of two starships and a handful of missiles is much easier than managing an equal number of massive stars. The combined mass of warring hardware is trivial compared with the mass of the central sun, and so the mutual gravitational attractions of ships and missiles are assumed to be zero. Given the distance of each object from the sun, TREK simply calculates the acceleration of the object caused by the centrally directed solar gravity, updates the velocity of the object and finally revises its position.

Even for such a conceptually simple calculation there is substantial computational overhead. Sums, products and square roots are needed to carry out each calculation. To avoid slowing down the game with excessive arithmetic, TREK consults a table; for every possible distance from the sun an array called *force* gives the predetermined acceleration experienced by an object (see Figure 8.3). Since the Star Trek universe is toroidal, the new position derived from the acceleration found in the *force* table must be calculated modulo the horizontal or vertical distance across the rectangular display.

Two arrays give the current velocity and position for the two starships and as many as 20 missiles; the arrays are called *vel* and *pos*. Each array has two columns and 22 rows. The first two rows hold starship data and the next 20 are devoted to missiles. Thus in the first row of *vel* the two entries *vel*(1,1) and *vel*(1,2) are respectively the velocities in the x (horizontal) direction and the y (vertical) direction of *Enterprise*. Similarly, *vel*(2,1) and *vel*(2,2) give the two mutually perpendicular velocity components of the Klingon battle cruiser. A special variable called *misnum* enables TREK to keep track of the number of missiles currently in flight. *Misnum* ranges from 2 (no missiles) through 22 (20 missiles).

By lumping starships and missiles together in the arrays one creates a shorter and slightly more efficient program. Only one loop is needed to update both positions and velocities. Before the update, however, two variables are needed to keep track of the orientations of the two spacecraft: *fdor* and *knor*. Their values are expressed in degrees, where the

DISTANCE	FORCE
10	8.000
11	6.612
12	5.556

$$\text{FORCE} = \frac{800}{(\text{DISTANCE})^2}$$

178	.025
179	.025
180	.025

Figure 8.3 Sample force table and its formula.

angle 0 indicates a ship is pointing east, 90 indicates north and so on. Every time a player presses either direction key, one of the two variables is increased or decreased by 10 degrees as appropriate.

The loop for updating positions is indexed by the letter i, which ranges from 1 through 22. For each value of i the program calculates the acceleration: the current values of the x and y coordinates of the ith row of *pos* are squared and added together. TREK then finds the square root of the sum, and that number is truncated to the greatest integer less than or equal to it. The truncated intetger square root is the approximate distance from the sun to the position of the ith object. That integer is then taken as an index to the acceleration table, where the solar attraction can be looked up.

For the two starships the components of solar acceleration must then be added to the components of thrust. If either flag variable *fdgo* or *kngo* has been set equal to 1 (in other words, if the thrust key has been pressed) and if neither starship is out of fuel, TREK must multiply the thrust constant by its horizontal and vertical components. For my monitor I take the thrust constant to be 3, which gives reasonable maneuverability to the spacecraft. For *Enterprise* the horizontal component is then three times the cosine of *fdor*; the vertical component is three times the sine of *fdor*. For the Klingon ship the thrust components are derived from the angle *knor*. As soon as the calculation is done TREK resets both *fdgo* and *kngo* to 0; the throttle is turned off until the next time the thrust key is pressed.

When the index *i* becomes greater than 2, the calculation of thrust can be bypassed because missiles have no thrust. The rest of the updating loop is devoted to calculating new velocities and positions for the moving objects on the screen. For each object the numerical magnitude of the acceleration is added to that of the velocity, and the magnitude of the velocity is added to that of the position. Such a simplistic calculation is made possible by adjusting the thrust and solar attraction to reflect a system of units that assumes the passage of one unit of time for each program cycle.

To check for contacts among the various objects the program must first determine for each ship whether the ship lies on or within the boundary of the sun. Since TREK has already calculated the updated distance between each ship and the sun, the program needs only to compare that distance with the solar radius, say 10 units. If either ship has collided with the sun, TREK responds with an appropriate screen message, such as KLINGON VAPORIZED; the program then branches to its display segment.

A second check for contact must determine for each missile whether the missile lies within a certain small distance of either ship. Here TREK uses a simple but effective shortcut: it finds the difference between the *x* coordinates of the missile and a ship, and it does the same for the two *y* coordinates. Finally it adds the two differences; the process avoids both squaring and taking square roots, and the result is nearly as good as the usual distance calculation. If the sum of the two differences is less than, say, 4, the program scores a hit. A message appears on the screen, such as ENTERPRISE HIT BY A MISSILE. KLINGON WINS. A single loop carries out the test for each missile. Its index starts at 3 and ends at *misnum*, the number of missiles in space plus 2.

To update the energy levels of the ships the program divides the solar acceleration obtained from the table by 60. Since the acceleration increases as the ship moves closer to the sun, such a ship can receive a more concentrated stream of energetic solar photons. The energy is then added to a fuel variable called *fdft* or *knfl*, depending on which starship is involved. Each of these variables is decreased by .1 when thrust is applied; the decrements are made in the position-updating segment of TREK. A starship is considered out of fuel if it has no more than one unit of solar energy left in its tank. The tank begins life with 10 units of fuel.

Missile management requires an array called *time*, which stores the number of program cycles in the life of each missile. When a cycle count reaches 25, the corresponding missile is removed from the array *pos*, the count is reset to 0 and *misnum* is decreased by 1. The missile can be removed from *pos* in one of two ways. The first method is easier to program but may slow down the game. TREK runs through the array from the index value at which the missile is removed and decreases the row number of each entry by 1. Thus the last entry to be shifted lies at index *misnum*. It is moved to row number *misnum*-1. The same operation is carried out on the arrays *vel* and *time*.

A faster technique takes advantage of the observation that the oldest missiles have the smallest indexes; they were the first missiles added to the list. One can therefore keep track of the missiles without shifting their indexes; missiles whose age has reached 25 program cycles must all be found at the beginning of a contiguous group of missiles in each array, and so only they must be removed. Similarly, new missiles are always added at the end of the contiguous group.

Introduce two new variables called *old* and *new*, which serve as pointers to the oldest and newest missiles in each array. As missiles are removed and added, only the values of *old* and *new* must be changed. One can then apply modular arithmetic to keep the contiguous group of missiles cycling around in each array. When a new missile is to be added at index value 23, TREK reduces the index modulo 23 to 0 and then adds 3 to avoid replacing one of the starship coordinates by a missile coordinate. The variables *old* and *new* undergo the same process. Such a data structure is called a circular queue. If this arcade trick is used, the position-updating segment of the program must be modified: split each single loop into two smaller loops, one for ships and the other for missiles.

When a player presses a key to fire a missile, TREK first checks a count of missiles currently activated by that side. If the count is less than 10, TREK consults the values of the flag variables *fdfr* and *knfr*. If *fdfr* is 1, for example, the program adds 1 to the missile count for the Federation, increases *misnum* by 1 and then loads the position and velocity coordinates of *Enterprise* into the appropriate slots of *pos* and *vel*. In the process the program should add four units to the position coordinates and two units to the velocity coordinates; in both cases the addition is made along the same direction as the ship is currently moving. For example, the horizontal position coordinate of a missile fired by *Enterprise* is four

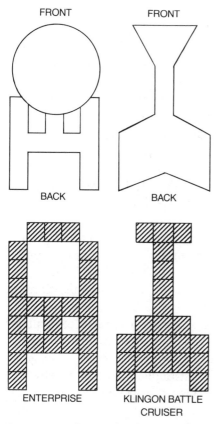

FRONT   FRONT

BACK   BACK

ENTERPRISE   KLINGON BATTLE
                          CRUISER

Figure 8.4 Icons (*top*) and their pixel versions.

times the cosine of *fdor* plus the horizontal position coordinate of *Enterprise*; the vertical coordinate increases by four times the sine of *fdor*. The initial position of the missile is thereby kept clear of the ship, preventing immediate destruction by the ship's own photon torpedo. The same operation applied to the missile's velocity coordinates reflects a relative launch speed of two units per cycle: a missile travels two units per cycle faster than the ship that launches it.

The last major section of TREK displays the sun, two ships and whatever missiles are active at a given time. The program draws a circle of radius 10 in the center of the screen and then works its way through the array *pos*. The Federation and Klingon ships are represented by icons. One icon is essentially a circle that recalls the famed discoidal *Enterprise* with its twin engine booms. The Klingon icon is angular (see Figure 8.4). Readers are free to attempt any miniature variation on these ships as long as two things are reasonably clear at a glance: which ship is which and where each one is headed. In drawing the icon for either spacecraft, TREK calls on a list of display points that must be translated and rotated to reflect the position and orientation of each object. For these operations the program consults the array *pos* and the variables *fdor* and *knor*.

Missiles are simpler. The display program draws each missile as a point within a single loop, consulting *pos* as it goes along.

TREK is subject to one disadvantage of the display screens now in popular use. Such screens operate in storage mode: an object drawn on the screen remains there. To avoid a confusing welter of remnant ships and missiles TREK must draw each object twice. It first draws the object in its old position in black. Then it redraws the object in its new position in the normal color.

I shall leave the details of initializing the program to the Trekkers who attempt it. In spite of arcade programming, some of you may find the game too slow; you may be tempted to call it Star Truck. For better performance try compiling your program, or impose arms limitations on the number of missiles allotted to each side.

I have described only the bare-bones version of Star Trek. Fancier but private editions have been built and they continue to propagate; games have appeared that allow three or more spacecraft, laser guns, color graphics and status displays. I must thank Jonathan N. Groff of Clearwater, Fla., for reminding me of this underground classic and for introducing me to a version of the game that includes an automated Klingon. Earthlings representing the Federation are continually wiped out by Groff's program.

9

WEATHER IN A JAR

The butterfly effect was the reason. For small pieces of
weather . . . prediction deteriorates rapidly. Errors
and uncertainties multiply . . .

JAMES GLEICK, *Chaos*

T he famed Lorenz attractor seems an apt symbol for the field of dynamics and chaos. Its gracefully interfolded wings remind us of the butterfly that flutters in Venezuela only to cause a typhoon in Taiwan. But how many readers know the arcana behind the Lorenz attractor, that it represents a miniature weather system confined to a jar? I will show how to simulate the system, not with Lorenz's differential equations, but with an equivalent dynamical system of equal fascination — Lorenz's water wheel.

James Gleick tells the story behind the Lorenz attractor in his book, *Chaos*. (See the Further Reading section at the end of this chapter.)

More than 30 years ago the MIT weather theorist Edward Lorenz constructed a primitive weather simulating program that ran on his Royal McBee computer, "a thicket of wiring and vacuum tubes that . . . broke down every week or so." The program incorporated equations that governed the interactions of air pressure, temperature, humidity, and so on. He would begin a run of his program by feeding numbers that represented meterological data at a number or "stations" throughout his miniature world. Then he would press the start key and the system would churn through the equations. Storms and calms fitted through the vacuum tubes as several "days" of weather passed. Then Lorenz would end the run. He was watching for consistencies in the data. If he could develop predictive methods with his ultra-simple weather simulation program, there might be hope for the real thing. He hardly expected that his model would hint so strongly in the other direction.

It happened one day when he typed in data for yet another run and went off for a coffee to let the Royal McBee buzz along on its own. When he came back to the office, he discovered to his horror that the run was for nothing. He had accidently omitted several decimal digits in the input numbers. A careful experimenter, Lorenz re-entered the data, fully expecting that the results of the more accurate numbers would differ very little (if at all) from those of the original run. He was astonished to find that the weather patterns prevailing in his miniature world at the end of the new run were completely different. He repeated both runs and got the same result. And again.

Searching for the reasons for the divergence, Lorenz refined and simplified his weather model. In the end it did not span the whole world, nor a single country, nor even a county. It consisted of a single convection cell. Such volumes are fairly common in weather systems: Warm air, heated by ground radiation rises. As it goes up the air cools. Could a single convection cell hold the key to strange behavior in his weather model?

Figure 9.1 shows a single cylindrical volume of circulating air. Heat applied at the bottom of the cylinder causes the central air to expand and rise, cooling as it goes. At the top of the cylinder, the air spreads out to the sides of the cylinder and begins to descend, cooling even more and completing the circulation. Lorenz used three differential equations to model events inside the convection cell. When he solved these by computer under different initial conditions and for different values of the parameter that represented the rate of heating, it did not take him long to discover an extraordinary phenomenon. In certain cases, a very slight change in the initial inputs would cause completely different behavior in the weather-in-a-jar system. The phenomenon now goes by the name "sensitivity to initial conditions." It is the hallmark of chaos.

The famous Lorenz attractor (Figure 9.1) summarizes all possible behaviors to which the weather-in-a-jar is "attracted" as it runs. The lines that wind around and around within the attractor represent trajectories in phase space, a three-dimensional space in which every point represents a unique combination of velocity, temperature, and rate of temperature change. As the computer solves the equations iteratively, the point moves through phase space. When the heat is turned up, so to speak, the point traces out the strange, nested curves of the Lorenz attractor. Here, you can see sensitivity to initial conditions explicitly. There are pairs of curves that pass arbitrarily close together within the

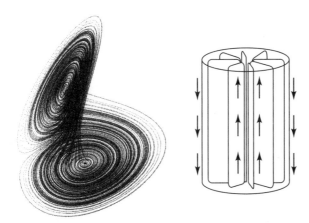

Figure 9.1 Weather in a jar and its attractor.

attractor's central portion, yet diverge to different wings of the butterfly. Within a short time, jar weathers that seem nearly identical develop in completely different ways.

To make your own Lorenzian weather model and watch it run, you do not have to build a little jar with air circulating inside it (although a French physicist did something very similar). Nor is it necessary to write a computer program that solves the three equations iteratively. All you have to do is write a program that mimics a certain water-wheel, a precise mechanical analog of weather in a jar.

Figure 9.2 shows a most peculiar water wheel in the act of turning. Eight leaky buckets hang from the wheel at evenly spaced points. Above the center of the wheel, a steady stream of water pours into each bucket as it swings underneath. Each bucket leaks at the same rate and, as it follows the wheel around, loses water.

The Lorenzian water wheel has no direct application that I am aware of — except to illustrate the behavior of the convection cell. Here, water is the analog of heat. Each bucket represents a portion of the cell's air that loses heat as it circulates within the cylinder. The analog does not suffer much from this discrete form of air and, provided there are enough buckets, the exact number is not important. The varying speed of the water wheel recreates the behavior of the air within the weather cell.

And what strange behavior it is! With water pouring slowly onto the wheel after a discreet clockwise nudge, it will rotate gently clockwise,

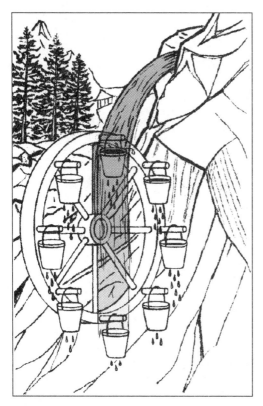

Figure 9.2 Lorenzian water wheel captures elementary weather dynamics.

speeding up to some limiting rotational velocity and maintaining it thereafter. But turn on the tap and let the water pour in. The wheel may speed up for a time, then mysteriously begin to slow, stop, and even reverse direction! Then it may (or may not) reverse direction again. The behavior seems random, even perverse. This is chaos. The reason for any particular behavior is never far to seek. If the wheel slows down and reverses, it is only because the buckets ascending the return side are fuller than those descending. The latter went by the tap more quickly.

Readers with a mechanical bent are of course free to build their own Lorenzian water wheel but others will resort to their computers, all on fire to see the wheel rotate.

The program I call WEATHER WHEEL captures the Lorenzian water wheel and its behavior within a computer. The eight buckets comprise an array by the same name and time passes in discrete steps that vary with the speed of the wheel. The algorithm in Figure 9.3 consists of four parts, an input segment, a dynamical computation segment, a relabelling segment, and a display segment.

The user of WEATHER WHEEL inputs the rate f at which water enters the system through the spout. The initial velocity v simply sets the wheel turning. Note that the initial velocity must be non-zero.

```
input filling rate f, leaking rate g
    input velocity v
    initialize buckets to 0 (empty)
repeat

***compute dynamics***
      dt ← abs(1/v)
      bucket(0) ← bucket(0) + f*dt
      for k ← 0 to 7
        if bucket(k)>=g*dt
            then bucket(k) ← bucket(k) − g*dt
            else bucket(k) ← 0
     rightwt ← 0
     for k ← 1 to 3
        rightwt ← rightwt + bucket(k)
     leftwt ← 0
     for k ← 5 to 7
        leftwt ← leftwt + bucket(k)
     acc ← (rightwt − leftwt)*const*dt
     v ← v + acc
     if v = 0 then v ← 0.001

     ***leak and relabel buckets***
     if v > 0 then inc ← +1
              else inc ← −1
     for k ← 0 to 7
        j ← (k + inc) mod 8
        bucket(j) ← bucket(k)

     ***display wheel***
     (display procedure)

until key pressed
```

Figure 9.3 Water wheel algorithm.

Inside the repeat loop a new state of the water wheel is computed on the basis of the previous state. The time constant dt reflects how quickly the wheel has been turning. It controls how long the top bucket (always labelled 0) will remain under the spout. Immediately, the top bucket receives $f*dt$ gallons (or any unit you want to imagine) of water.

Before the wheel turns in this discrete rotational world, the buckets must all leak a little. A loop runs through all eight buckets, removing a quantity of water that is proportional to the leak rate g applied over the time interval dt. Next, contributions to any change in velocity must be computed by adding up the weights of the three right-hand buckets and those of the three left-hand buckets. The acceleration, a, will be the difference between the two weights multiplied by some constant, *const*, and again by dt, the period over which the acceleration will act. Readers may want to start with *const* $= 1$ and then alter it later, if necessary. WEATHER WHEEL next updates the velocity by adding the acceleration increment. This step is kosher if I argue that the constant that would otherwise multiply *acc* has been absorbed by the units chosen.

Because the time increment uses $1/v$, the program must prevent v from becoming 0 by testing for this condition and then making it slightly non-zero, if necessary. The generation of a 0 by the program is highly unlikely, but possible.

It may seem eccentric to relabel the buckets but that simplifies the programming somewhat. The alternative involves a rather messy computation of which buckets currently contribute to the right-hand and which to the left-hand weights. But watch the modular arithmetic! It requires that the index values for the bucket array start at 0. Depending on which way the wheel happens to be turning (v is positive or negative), the contents of each bucket are transferred, in effect, to its clockwise or counter-clockwise neighbor.

The display procedure opens up a host of possibilities. At a minimum, any decent graphic rendering will show eight apparently stationary buckets with differing amounts of water circulating one way or the other. Each bucket may be represented by a square in which either a) a number representing the current contents is printed, or b) a special "fill" routine covers the lower area of the square to an appropriate height with graphic water. Two options enter the picture in this case: How much water should buckets be allowed to hold?

Readers who place no limits on bucket capacity must, nevertheless, limit the graphic fill to the top of each bucket. Readers who limit the amount in their programs will not face this problem. On the one hand, the heat capacity of air is theoretically unlimited and so should the capacity of buckets be. But I suspect it will not make any difference which option one pursues except at very high fill rates.

One final and crucial piece of advice for the display section: Add a timing loop that freezes the display for a period of time that is proportional to *dt*. This will slow the simulation down, of course, but only in a physically realistic way. Who wants to watch the Lorenzian wheel "spinning" always at the same rate? The timing loop holds up the program by executing some trivial or pointless instruction while it counts toward the loop limit, int(1000*dt*). If the 1000 factor does not produce an appropriate increment, it may be increased or decreased by factors of 10. 258177

This brings to mind some related issues concerning physical simulations. I have played fast and loose with the physics of the Lorenzian water wheel. Consider what happens in the algorithm: The wheel is essentially stationary while water is added to the top bucket and then leaked out of all the buckets. Then the weight contributions are calculated to produce a new wheel speed and the buckets all move, in effect, to their next positions. The newly calculated speed determines how long the top bucket will fill and all the buckets will leak during the next cycle of computation. All of this seems reasonable if you imagine that during each cycle the wheel turns steadily at precisely the predetermined rate, v. During that period, the top bucket will receive exactly the amount computed. And during that period some of the buckets, at least, may well leak the amount of water so computed. Unfortunately, real leakage (like real heat loss) is proportional to the amount present. I have not built this into the model on the assumption that it makes little or no difference. Careful simulators may want to alter the loss from "g*dt" to "bucket(k)*dt", allowing the constant g to alter its meaning.

These simplifications, due mainly to the discrete nature of the model, will nevertheless allow chaos to appear. Readers with a yen to explore sensitivity to initial conditions may experiment by isolating what they suspect to be chaotic behavior, having made a careful note of the initial conditions that led to it. Now alter those conditions by however slight an amount. Does a similar scenario evolve or an entirely different one?

Further Reading

James Gleick. *CHAOS Making a New Science.* Viking, 1987.

10

A Portrait of Chaos

I feel that art has something to do with the achievement of stillness in the midst of chaos.

SAUL BELLOW

While investigating digestion, Mario Markus of the Max Planck Institute for Nutrition discovered beauty in chaos. He and his collaborator Benno Hess have studied several mathematical models in an attempt to simulate how enzymes break down carbohydrates. By adjusting a pair of parameters, they found they could make the simulated enzymes behave in either an orderly or chaotic manner. To illustrate the chaos inherent in the model, Markus created a series of portraits of chaos that provided not only food for thought but also a feast for the eyes.

The images are based on a formula named after the Russian mathematician Aleksandr M. Lyapunov. The formula generates a single number for any dynamic system. Known as the Lyapunov exponent, the number indicates how chaotically the system is behaving. When the Lyapunov formula is applied to Markus's model, it produces an exponent for each pair of parameters. By representing each pair as a point on a computer screen and assigning colors to each point depending on the value of the exponent, Markus created what I call Lyapunov space. In this virtually unexplored territory, order inhabits colored shapes, and chaos lurks in black regions.

Not long after his work appeared in academic journals, Markus rushed several pictures to an art gallery for exhibition. He can hardly be blamed for doing so. The pictures could just as easily have been made by an apprentice to Salvador Dali.

The model developed by Markus is based on a variation of the so-called logistic formula, the simplest-known formula that describes a chaotic dynamic system. The formula contains a variable, x, whose value is always somewhere between 0 and 1. It also involves a system parameter, r. The formula can be written:

$$x \leftarrow rx(1 - x)$$

The arrow indicates that once r, x, and $1 - x$ have all been multiplied together, the resulting number becomes the new value for x, that is, it replaces the old value. The process can be repeated so that the formula continually spews out new values for x.

The resulting sequence holds great fascination for dynamicists, but what does it all mean? The logistic equation gets its name from the logistics of animal populations. In the equation, x represents the number of animals in an isolated region divided by the maximum number that the region could ever be expected to support. The amount of food available is therefore proportional to $1 - x$. In other words, as the number of animals (x) approaches the maximum (1), the food supply ($1 - x$) dwindles to nothing (0). The parameter r expresses the proportionality. It may be thought of as the fecundity of the population. The higher the value of r, the more quickly the population will rebound from any disaster. Strangely enough, higher values are precisely the ones that lead most quickly to chaotic populations.

Although the equation is too simple to represent real animal populations, it can serve as a rough approximation to population dynamics.

If the parameter r is less than 2, the sequence of numbers produced quickly homes in on a single value. It makes no difference what number the formula uses for x initially. The population always converges to a stable value. In the jargon of chaos theory, a system whose dynamics stabilize at a single value is said to have a one-point attractor.

If the parameter r is greater than 2 but less than about 2.45, the logistic formula generates numbers, that eventually alternate between two values. The system then converges on a two-point attractor. In some sense, when fecundity is high, the population pays a price: its size fluctuates over time.

If the fecundity factor is cranked up to values greater than 2.45, the logistic formula produces numbers that converge on a four-point attractor. Still higher values of r lead very quickly to eight-point attractors, then 16-point ones and so on. But if the value of r is greater than 3.57 (or, to be more precise, 3.56994571869), chaos reigns.

At that level of fecundity, the formula seems to generate values at random, though, to be sure, the formula is deterministic. The reason for this strange behavior lies in the attractor. It happens to be a one-dimensional fractal. Like all fractals, it is self-similar: when any small piece of it is magnified, the enlarged region looks very much like the whole.

The fate of the hypothetical populations is clearly portrayed in Figure 10.1. The diagram is produced by plotting r against the values to which the logistic formula converges. The result is a kind of tree. One-point attractors make up the trunk; two-point attractors, the first pair of branches. At an r value of 3.57, the onset of chaos can be seen clearly: the branches suddenly proliferate.

Chaos can be characterized using the Lyapunov formula. For each dynamic system, the formula produces a single number, the Lyapunov exponent. If the number is less than 0, the system is stable. If the number is greater than 0, the system is capable of chaotic behavior.

The Lyapunov formula is complicated, but it can be translated into a series of simple steps. In the case of the logistic system, we start with one particular value of r. The logistic formula is iterated, say, 600 times, so that the numbers converge to whatever attractor is present in the system. After the numbers settle down, it is safe to compute the Lyapunov exponent. The following recipe outlines the computation:

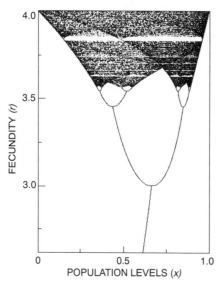

Figure 10.1 Population levels, x, can fluctuate over a wider range of values as the fecundity factor, r, increases.

```
total ← 0
for n ← 1 to 4,000
    x ← rx(1 − x)
    total ← total + ((log|r − 2rx|)/log 2)
lyap ← total/4,000
```

The algorithm first sets *total* = 0 and then iterates the logistic formula 4,000 times. On each iteration it computes a new value for *total* by adding the old value of *total* to the logarithm of $|r − 2rx|$ divided by the logarithm of 2. (The vertical bars indicate the absolute value of $r − 2rx$.) The quantity $|r − 2rx|$ represents the magnitude of the rate at which successive values are growing or shrinking. When it has added up all 4,000 logarithms, the algorithm divides the sum by 4,000. The result, which has been assigned to the variable *lyap* above, is something like an average logarithm of change. The result closely approximates the Lyapunov exponent.

Readers who demand precision can more accurately estimate the Lyapunov exponent by increasing the number of iterations and, at the end of the procedure, by dividing the sum of logarithms by the number of iterations.

I encourage readers to use the algorithm above to calculate the Lyapunov exponent for *r* equal to 3. Then compare the result with that obtained when *r* equals 3.57. The first number should be slightly negative, indicating a stable system, and the second number should be positive, a warning of chaos.

Figures 10.2 through 10.4 are all based on the logistic equation. Markus merely adds one twist of his own. To produce his pictures, Markus used periodic forcing. This means that *r* systematically changes its value, alternating between two fixed numbers, *a* and *b*. In other words, the logistic equation is iterated with *r* values of *a*, then *b*, *a*, *b*, *a*, *b* and so on. The resulting system may or may not develop chaotic behavior. The issue can be settled only by calculating the Lyapunov exponent.

For that reason, Markus plotted the value of the exponent for each possible combination of *a* and *b* values. A two-dimensional image in Lyapunov space emerges when the points (*a*, *b*) are colored in some consistent fashion. Markus assigned black to all points (*a*, *b*) that produce a non-negative value for the Lyapunov exponent. Chaos is black. Shades of a single color, such as yellow, appear everywhere else in Lyapunov space. From a Lyapunov exponent of zero down to minus infinity, the

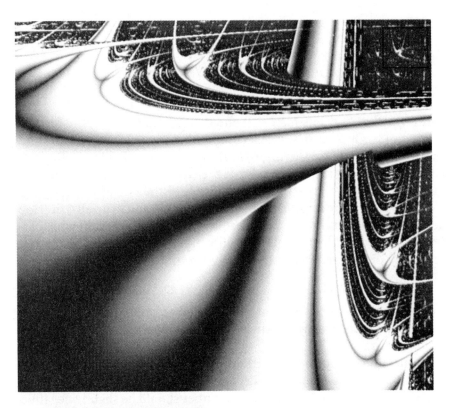

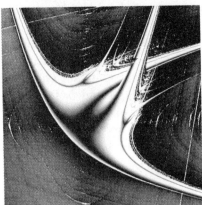

Figure 10.2 Lyapunov space (*above*) and a detail (*below*) showing the "swallow."

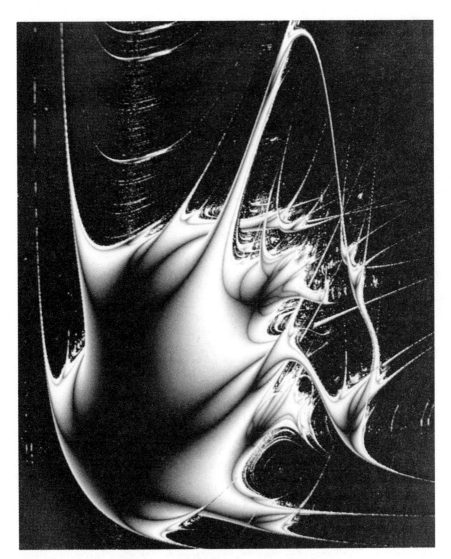

Figure 10.3 A Lyapunov ''jellyfish.''

shade ranges continuously from light to dark. At zero, there is an abrupt discontinuity as the color suddenly turns from bright yellow to black.

The resulting images are maps of chaos in the forced logistic system. In particular, the upper image in Figure 10.2 depicts the straightforward system just described. The parameter r alternates in completely regular fashion between a and b.

Figure 10.4 Zircon Zity.

The crossing point of two or more spikes in any of the accompanying images reveals the coexistence of periodic attractors. This means that, at a point (a, b) where such a crossing occurs, the corresponding dynamic system in which r alternates between a and b will have two attractors. Which attractor operates depends, strangely enough, on the initial value that one chooses for x before iteration.

If the Lyapunov exponent is plotted for a succession of initial x values, it may take on a specific value, say, 0.015 for a number of these initial values. Then the exponent may suddenly switch to another value, 0.142, to which it may stick for several more successive initial x values before reverting to the first value. The switching back and forth can become quite frequent.

Lyapunov space often contains darkish bands that run along the spikes. These represent superstable regions in which the underlying forced logistic systems exhibit the most regular behavior.

The Lyapunov space generated by alternating a and b values contains a tiny fleck that resembles a swallow. The fleck is enlarged in the image at the bottom of Figure 10.2. There, just off the swallow's tail, lies another little fleck. Readers are free to guess just what it might turn out to be when it is similarly enlarged.

The appearance of self-similarity in the figure should not surprise students of chaos. Structures that exhibit self-similarity are more often than not produced by chaotic processes.

The methods used to create the mother swallow and its offspring can be varied slightly to generate a host of different creatures. The images in Figures 10.3 and 10.4 differ only in the *a* and *b* value sequences that were used. For example, a jellyfish—the yellow tentacled blob shown in Figure 10.3—is spawned from a sequence that begins *b, b, a, b, a* and that repeats over and over again.

Figure 10.4 resembles the cover of a science fiction magazine from the 1950s. I call it Zircon Zity because it is obviously the futuristic metropolis of the Zirconites (whoever they are). The underlying sequence of the zity is *bbbbbbaaaaaa*. By repeating this sequence while calculating the Lyapunov exponent, a computer can build the city with all its delicate bridges, golden spaceships, and interplanetary walkways.

What does all this have to do with enzymes, carbohydrates, and nutrition? At best, a small region in some Lyapunov map might actually describe the dynamics of enzymes breaking down carbohydrates. But perhaps more to the point, Markus's work makes it possible to visualize the dynamics of periodic forcing. One might say he has made chaos easier to digest.

A Lyapunov Program

For those readers who wish to explore Lyapunov space, I can give a few hints about how they might create the appropriate program. The heart of the program should be a double loop that runs through values of *a* and *b*. To compute the Lyapunov exponent for each combination of *a* and *b*, the program should include a routine based on the algorithm given on page 103. The routine should allow various sequences of *a*'s and *b*'s to be stored in an array. The routine could enable the user to specify the sequence by filling the array with 0's (representing *a*) and 1's (representing *b*).

With each iteration of the Lyapunov loop, a counter called *index* may be used to step through the array. Each time the inner loop produces a new value for *index*, it will look up the current value of either *a* or *b*, depending on whether it finds a 0 or a 1 in the array at the value of *index*. Finally, the program should include a table of logarithms to help speed the computations. Indeed, it may take hours for a personal computer to generate a single image in Lyapunov space.

Further Reading

A. K. Dewdney. *The Magic Machine: A Handbook of Computer Sorcery.* W. H. Freeman, 1990.

Mario Markus. "Chaos in Maps with Continuous and Discontinuous Maxima." *Computers in Physics,* September/October 1990, pp. 481–493.

11

DESIGNER FRACTALS

So, naturalists observe, a flea Hath smaller fleas that
on him prey; And these have smaller still to bite 'em;
And so proceed *ad infinitum.*

JONATHAN SWIFT, *On Poetry. A Rhapsody*

So, mathematicians observe, if fleas are all the same except for size, then all their hopping and rotations reduce to affine transformations. What exactly is this high-sounding term? It is nothing more than a formula for scaling, turning, displacing, and sometimes even distorting an object geometrically. As in the case of fleas, a single affine transformation can be applied repeatedly to produce miniature replicas of the original. People who prefer not to waste their talents on propagating fleas can apply these rather simple geometric formulas to generate images as intricate as the paintings in museums or landscapes in nature.

A small set of affine transformations can create such abstract works as the Sierpinski triangle in Figure 11.1. A larger group of transformations can re-create landscapes such as the Monterey coastline shown in Figure 11.2. In fact, any image whatsoever can be reproduced from a series of affine transformations. The trick is knowing which ones to choose. Along these lines, Michael F. Barnsley of Iterated Systems, Inc., in Norcross, Ga., has discovered a general procedure for reducing an image into a series of affine transformations. His technique has opened up some exciting possibilities for the transmission of television and computer images. Before I describe his work, let me say a bit more about affine transformations.

When an affine transformation is applied to a figure such as a triangle or a leaf, it moves the points that make up the figure to new locations. In the process, the transformation may translate, scale, rotate, and stretch

Figure 11.1 The Sierpinski triangle.

the original figure. If one starts with a triangle, an affine transformation could shrink the triangle and move it to the left somewhat, thus creating a second triangle. If the same transformation is applied to the smaller, displaced triangle, it will produce a third triangle that bears the same relation in size and proximity to the second triangle as the second does to the first. One can apply the transformation repeatedly and watch the triangles trace a path into infinitesimal oblivion.

If one applies an infinite series of affine transformations to an object, the result has the property of being self-similar, that is, a magnified portion of the result looks like the whole. Hence, a series of affine transformations can create a self-similar object, better known as a fractal.

All affine transformations have the same kind of formula for moving the points of a figure around in a plane. The original point can be defined by two coordinates, which I will call x and y. The new point has the coordinates (x', y'). The transformation is then defined by two equations:

$$x' = ax + by + e$$
$$y' = cx + dy + f$$

The symbols a, b, c, d, e, and f represent a set of numbers that determine the character of the affine transformation.

What would happen, for example, if b were equal to .5, c were $-.5$ and a, d, e and f were all 0? The two equations that define the affine transformation would become:

Figure 11.2 Photograph of Monterey coastline (*top*) and the same image (*bottom*) reproduced from a few affine transformations.

$$x' = .5\,y$$
$$Y' = -\,.5\,x$$

To determine its effect on a specific point, say (1, 2), one merely applies the formulas. Thus, x' becomes (.5 $\times$ 2), which equals 1, and similarly y' becomes $-$ .5. If one carries out this operation for a great many points in a triangle, a general pattern emerges. The entire triangle seems to have rotated 90 degrees clockwise and simultaneously to have shrunk to half its former size. If e and f were both equal to 1 instead of 0, then not only would the triangle be reduced and rotated, it would also be shifted one whole unit up and to the right.

This kind of transformation is called contractive because its effect on any collection of points is to shrink the distances between them. The transformation also preserves shapes. Contraction and shape preservation are key properties of the affine transformations employed in the technique that Barnsley calls an iterated-function system.

The fun begins when several transformations of this kind are applied many times to any figure the mind can imagine. The transformations, along with their continued reapplication, make up an iterated-function system. One might think initially that solving the formulas for iterated-function systems involves an extraordinary amount of arithmetic. For instance, if a sequence of transformations were applied to a figure composed of 1,000 points, each transformation would have to operate on 1,000 points at a time. This would yield 8,000 arithmetic operations.

The astute reader will realize that to determine the effect of an iterated-function system on a figure such as a triangle, it is necessary to operate only on the three corner points. (The figure can be completed by simply connecting the points with lines.) In this case the transformation would only have to operate on three points at a time, and yet no savings can be guaranteed for a figure that has an irregular shape whose outline is defined by many points.

Do not despair. Barnsley has come up with a clever idea so that even complicated figures can be efficiently transformed many times. The advantage of his technique is that only one point at a time is transformed. His idea can be appreciated by playing the game I call fractal tennis.

This unusual racket sport requires four mathematically minded players and an umpire. The players — Abby, Bob, Carla and David — stand around a square court, separated by two nets that divide the court into four square quadrants. The umpire assigns each player to a home quadrant. To start the game, the umpire tosses a ball into Abby's home quadrant and shouts "Bob." Abby lets the ball bounce only once, swings her racket and hits the ball over the net so that it lands in Bob's quadrant.

Abby is not allowed to hit the ball to just anywhere in Bob's quadrant, however. To make the perfect shot as prescribed by the rules, she must first judge where the ball landed in her own quadrant. This task is rather simple because the tennis ball, which has been soaked in black ink, leaves a mark on the court. Abby creates a mental map of the ink mark within the entire court. She superposes the map on Bob's home quadrant by shrinking it to half its dimensions. The position of the superposed ink mark on Bob's quadrant is where she must hit the ball. If the ball had landed in the center of the whole court, Abby would have been required to hit the ball to the center of Bob's quadrant. In this case, however, the ball landed two meters north and six meters west of the center of the whole court. Because the dimensions of Bob's quadrant and the others are half those of the court as a whole, Abby should hit the ball one meter north and three meters west of the center of Bob's quadrant.

Abby's great shot represents an affine transformation. She has created a second ink mark, which has been displaced to Bob's quadrant and is closer to its boundaries.

After Abby's return, the umpire calls out "David." Bob rushes to catch the ball on the bounce and makes a perfect shot into David's home quadrant. The umpire, perhaps a bit maddened by the sun, then starts to shout names at random. Yet Abby, Bob, Carla, and David, being consummate calculators, play a flawless game. Each player always hits the ball to just the right point. After a while, however, the ink marks left by the tennis ball create a fractal pattern on the court. In fact, the marks eventually blacken the court uniformly. That is when the umpire calls a halt to the play.

Figure 11.3 shows the early stages of the game. After Bob made his first shot to David, the umpire called "David" for a second time. This did not present a problem, except for David of course. He hit the ball toward the southeast corner of his own quadrant because his quadrant is in the southeast corner of the whole court. After the ball bounced in David's own quadrant, the umpire called "Carla," and David hit the ball to her quadrant according to the rules. If the umpire had yelled "David" again and again, David would have had to direct the ball ever closer to the southeast corner.

Fractal tennis illustrates a key feature of iterated-function systems. A single point mapped repeatedly by a random sequence of affine trans-

THE UMPIRE SHOUTS

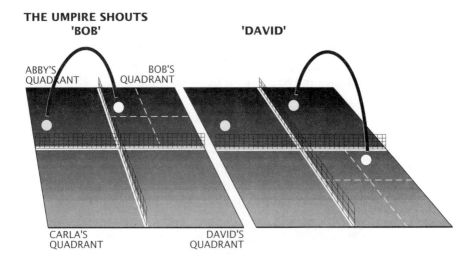

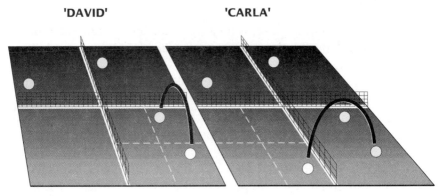

Figure 11.3 Opening shots in a game of fractal tennis.

formations will eventually "fill in" a certain region. The umpire's calls, or transformations, are what determine the ultimate image. In practice, the game ends when a satisfactory density of black dots emerges.

Readers who wonder why the game is called "fractal" tennis will see the game come into its own when it is played on the leaf of a black spleenwort fern. The game still involves four players, but unlike the classic smooth square of the practice court, the fern-leaf court has a jagged outline. As Figure 11.3 shows, when the umpire calls "Abby," one of the players must hit the ball to Abby's leaflet. The point where the ball must land depends on the position of the last bounce relative to the whole leaf. In this way, the call "Abby" corresponds to an affine transformation. The call "Bob" is also an affine transformation that sends the "ball" to the corresponding point in the leaflet at the left side of the leaf near the base. The call "Carla" does the same thing in relation to the leaflet at the right side of the base. Finally, the call "David" sends any point of the leaf as a whole into the straightline segment representing the stem at the base of the leaf.

When the point is put into play, the umpire begins to call the names of these four players in a random order. The point might start in the middle of the leaf, hop to the middle of Bob's leaflet, then shift to a point in Carla's leaflet and so on. The game goes on for 10,000 hits. As it continues, an image of the fern leaf, delicate and organic-looking, emerges (see Figure 11.4).

There is one element of the game that I have yet to describe. The sequence is not quite random: the judge favors certain players as he makes the 10,000 calls. The case of the spleenwort leaf provides a perfect example. Abby's leaflet has the largest area. Therefore, if the umpire is just as likely to shout "Abby" as any of the other three names, Abby's leaflet will fill in more slowly than the others'. To adjust for this, the umpire gives Abby the lion's share of play. In fact, the amount is proportional to Abby's share of the total leaf area.

The umpire calls "Bob" and "Carla" roughly the same number of times, the numbers in both cases being proportional to the areas of their respective leaflets. Because the stem has the least area of all, David will get to play the least.

Perceptive readers may have noticed that the four transformations associated with the spleenwort leaf change the basic outline into four re-

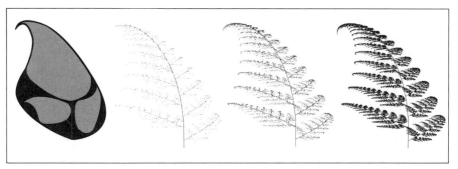

Figure 11.4 An iterated-function system fills in the leaf of a black spleenwort fern.

gions that approximately subdivide the outlined area. Barnsley calls this subdivision a collage. He and his colleagues have found a theorem that guarantees good fractal reproduction. The collage theorem says that the more accurately the outline of a fractal shape is approximated by a collage of a certain number of affine transformations of the shape, the more accurately the iterated-function system will reproduce the original fractal.

The collage theorem brings us to a fork in the expository road, that between creation and re-creation. To what purpose will an iterated-function system be put?

Creatively speaking, almost any fractal can be constructed by means of one iterated-function system or another. Take, for example, the Sierpinski triangle shown in Figure 11.1. This is a triangle from which a central triangular area has been removed, leaving three smaller triangles. Given the fractal nature of our topic, it will surprise no reader to find that each of the three triangles has its own central triangle removed.

Three affine transformations participate in the production of the Sierpinski triangle. They arise from a collage composed of three identical right triangles that all have the same orientation. The triangles in the collage are positioned to form a right triangular hole of the same size as one of the three triangles. Each of the triangles is associated with a particular affine transformation. When the game of fractal tennis is played on this strange surface, the original triangle begins to fill in, except for the hole in its middle. Each of the corner triangles has a hole in its middle, of course, and so do the triangles in their "corners." The final object, insofar as any finite scheme can reproduce it, is literally full of triangular holes at all visible scales of magnitude.

Readers who have computers at their command can reproduce the Sierpinski triangle by following an algorithm for the appropriate iterated-function system. I will describe the algorithm in general terms. It begins by setting the coordinates x and y equal to 0. Then three main operations are repeated 10,000 times: First, one of the affine transformations is chosen at random. Second, the chosen affine transformation is applied to the current coordinates of the point, namely, (x, y). The result is a set of new values that are now deposited in the x and y symbols, so to speak. Third, a test is made to determine whether 10 iterations have been carried out.

The third step ensures that the ball has been in play long enough to be somewhere in the court. In a general scheme such as this, one does not know in advance the best place to start the ball bouncing. Hence, one starts it from the origin and assumes that after 10 iterations it has pretty well "settled into" regular play.

This algorithm will work for any iterated-function system if one adds an extra feature. Because an affine transformation must be chosen at a rate that depends on the area it must cover, the algorithm must select each transformation with a certain probability.

What are the formulas for the affine transformations that produce the Sierpinski triangle? At the beginning of this chapter, I described the type of formula one needs, and I mentioned that six coefficients determine the transformation's character. The coefficients for the Sierpinski triangle are given below.

	a	b	c	d	e	f
(1)	.5	0	0	.5	0	0
(2)	.5	0	0	.5	.5	0
(3)	.5	0	0	.5	.5	.5

Each row of the table represents one of the three transformations.

One can tell what these particular transformations are up to almost at a glance. All three have the primary effect of shrinking any geometric figure to half its size, but transformation number 1 also shrinks the figure toward the origin, whereas transformations 2 and 3 move the shrunken form one unit to the right and one-half unit up and to the right, respectively. Thus, the original triangle is transformed into three smaller triangles, and the miniature triangles are in turn transformed into minuscule ones.

From these simple ingredients, readers with moderate programming experience should be able to reconstruct the Sierpinski triangle on their display screens.

Up to this point I have addressed the creation of forms. There is not as much recreation in re-creation, but that is the major application of iterated-function systems. Thanks to Barnsley and his colleagues it is now possible to convert any scene into an iterated-function system.

Normally it takes thousands of bits of information to store the image of a natural scene in a computer file. For example, an image might consist of a 300-by-300 grid of pixels, or picture elements, each requiring several bits to specify a gray level or color at that point. Ordinary pixel-by-pixel storage might therefore take up a million bits or more. One can apply standard compression techniques to such pictorial data to store the same information in a smaller space, but iterated-function systems promise compression factors of 500 to 1 — or even better! The key: store the iterated-function system rather than the image it produces. A glance at the pictures of the Monterey coastline in Figure 11.2 enables one to compare the veracity of the coded image (on the right) with the original photograph (on the left).

The method begins with a computer image drawn directly from a photograph or video camera. The image is analyzed and broken up into connected patches, large and small, in which the gray level (or color) is relatively constant. The pieces in this collage become the basis for a search through a large library of standard affine transformations that map some pieces into others. If it should happen, for example, that one of the transformations maps a droplet of spray into a great many other droplets, then that transformation would make a valuable addition to the iterated-function system under construction. Actual images can then be reconstructed in certain computers at video rates, that is, faster than 30 whole images per second.

The commercial potential of the discovery so impressed Alan D. Sloan, a mathematician formerly at the Georgia Institute of Technology and a close collaborator of Barnsley's, that the two researchers started Iterated Systems. Among the company's current products is a video modem that produces an iterated-function-system code for a 512-by-512 pixel image in just under three seconds. At the receiving end the images can be reconstructed at video rates. In the future Barnsley sees full-color video transmission over telephone lines as a definite possibility. The technology may also be applied to automated pattern recognition and other projects that are as yet a fractal gleam in Barnsley's eye.

Further Reading

Michael F. Barnsley. *Fractals Everywhere.* Academic Press, 1988.
Benoit B. Mandelbrot. *The Fractal Geometry of Nature.* W. H. Freeman, 1983.

12

THE FRACTAL WORKSHOP

The number of distinct scales of length of natural
patterns is for all practical purposes infinite.

BENOIT B. MANDELBROT, *The Fractal Geometry of Nature*

Since Benoit B. Mandelbrot first coined the term, we have learned to look for fractals everywhere, especially in nature. Although nature contains no true fractals, in which every part contains an infinite regress of similar parts, it abounds with structures that produce the illusion. One may find self-similar structure in certain leaves and plants, in shorelines, perhaps even in the structure of galaxies and galactic clusters. But a chapter on the elements of fractal generation may as well practice on the traditional elements of nature: earth, air, fire and water.

Earth may be symbolized by a jagged mountain, air by a puffy fractal cloud, fire by a fractal flame and water by an infinitely curly wave. Air and water are shown in Figures 12.1 and 12.3 but readers can supply earth and fire for themselves, based on what they glean from this chapter.

Chapter 11, which describes the iterated function systems (IFS) of Michael F. Barnsley and his co-worker Alan D. Sloan, makes the method clear but provides little in the way of concrete details.

A set of simple equations and an iteration rule that uses them sends a point hopping madly about the plane. If the point is plotted in each of its successive positions, thousands of them in fact, a fractal image slowly fills in. In this chapter readers will find an algorithmic description that is complete enough to begin programming: you may float away on a fractal cloud or ride a fractal wave. Such is the power of computers!

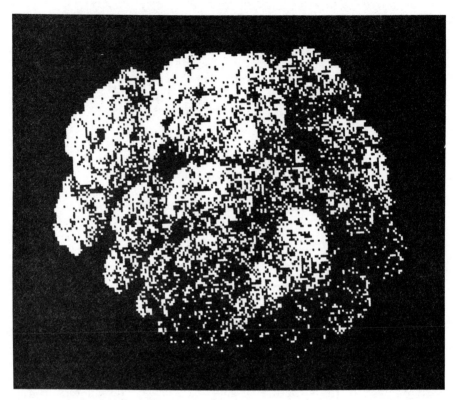

Figure 12.1 An IFS produces a fractal cloud.

Suppose you have a description of a fractal object (whether real or fanciful) in the form of a map. The object will normally be composed of parts, each similar to the whole. The first step in setting up an iterated function system, or IFS, is to prepare by hand what Barnsley calls a "collage." This is essentially a map of the object as a region which is divided into sub-regions that are similar to the region as a whole. Consider, for example, the upper collage shown in Figure 12.2. Here, the region that represents the circular outline of a cloud as a whole has been subdivided into six sub-cloud regions.

The next step in the preparation of the program is to set up what mathematicians call affine transformations, one for each part of the whole. In the case of the cloud and its six sub-clouds, six affine transformations are called for. Each transformation has three parts: A shrinkage of the original cloud down to the size of the sub-cloud, a rotation of the

Color Plate 1 Early model of the Tinkertoy computer,
on display at The Computer Museum, Boston,
also plays tic-tac-toe.

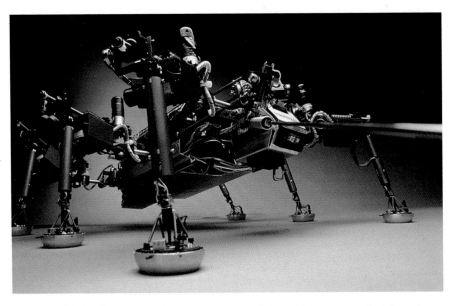

Color Plate 2   Insectoid prototype Genghis strides over rock (above),
production model Hannibal awaits action (below).

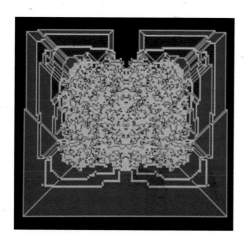

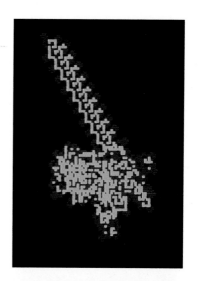

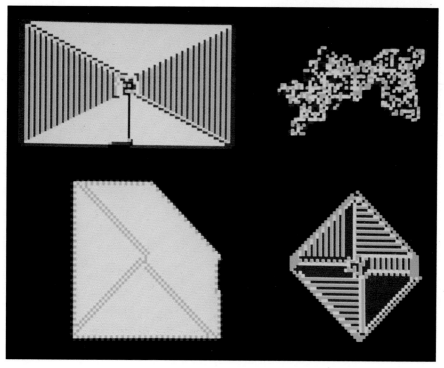

Color Plate 3   Patterns demonstrate the amazing variety of tur-mite behaviors

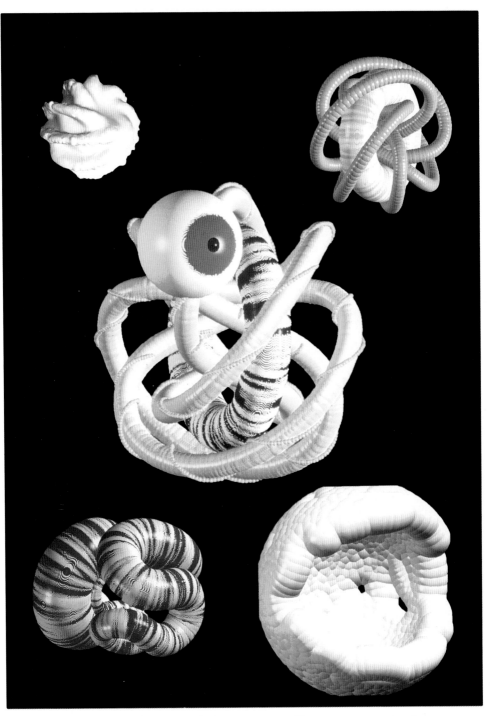

Color Plate 4   A zoo of alien creatures illustrates some simple
graphic tricks.

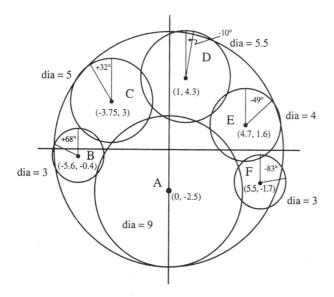

Figure 12.2 Working collage for a cloud.

sub-cloud, then a translation (shift) of the sub-cloud into its target position. The effect of such a transformation is to move any point in the big cloud into the corresponding point of the sub-cloud. Thus a point near the top of the big cloud will end up close to the top of the sub-cloud.

To set up an affine transformation, you must first determine a reasonable coordinate system, one that makes the transformations simple. By placing the origin at the center of the big cloud, the transformations are easy to obtain, especially if the exercise is carried out on graph paper. At the end of this chapter, I will explain exactly how I obtained them. The general form of an affine transformation is:

$$x' \leftarrow ax + by + e \quad \text{and}$$
$$y' \leftarrow cx + dy + f$$

The values of a, b, c, d, e, and f are best presented in a table. For the cloud the table has six rows, one for each sub-cloud in the collage. The sub-clouds are labelled with capital letters that have nothing to do with lower case letters just mentioned. For each sub-cloud, naturally, there is

a corresponding transformation that maps the whole cloud into that particular sub-cloud:

	a	b	c	d	e	f
A	.643	0	0	.643	0	−2.5
B	.08	−.199	.199	.08	−5.6	−0.4
C	.303	−.189	.189	.303	−3.7	3.0
D	.386	−.068	.068	.386	1	4.3
E	.187	.754	−.754	.187	4.7	1.6
F	.026	.213	−.213	.026	3.5	−1.7

It is a simple matter to produce two equations from each line of the
table. Simply substitute the values of a, b, and e into the first equation
and the values of c, d, and f into the second one. I have used the algorithmic replacement symbol ($\leftarrow$) in place of an equals because that is how a
fractal-generating program must ultimately use these numbers. Inciden-
tally, I have placed the symbols x' and y' on the left-hand sides of these
equations instead of x and y. The reason lies in the preservation of information during a computation. If I used x and y instead of x' and y', the
program would destroy the old value of x before the second equation got
to use it. Once both equations have been computed, the program may
replace old values by new values by using the following simple assignments:

$$x \leftarrow x'$$
$$y \leftarrow y'$$

In any event, the coordinates (x, y) represent a point before it is
moved and the coordinates (x', y') represent the point after a particular
transformation has moved it.

Once we have set up the transformations for an IFS, we may set a
point in motion by an iterative process; wherever the point happens currently to be, the process will plot it, then move it to a new location within
the cloud as a whole. In the collage that we will use, the sub-clouds are
represented by circles of different sizes. In most IF systems, the iterative
process sends a point in the object as a whole into a sub-object with a
probability that corresponds to the sub-object's area. In the case of the
cloud, it turned out (by calculating the area of each circle, then reducing
all the numbers proportionally until they added to 1) that the resulting
probabilities must be:

A: .47, B: .06, C: .15,
D: .18, E: .09, F: .05

Unfortunately, the use of these probabilities results in a cloud that looks too bottom-heavy. To compensate, I greatly reduced the probability of a point landing in the large sub-cloud at the bottom of the collage. Giving cloud A a probability of .21 instead of .47, the result was definitely more cloud-like. Readers should feel equally free to tinker with the probabilities to obtain different effects.

At the toss of an abstract coin, the program selects one of the sub-clouds and maps the current point (x, y) into it by means of the appropriate transformation. Each of the transformations shrinks the large cloud down to the size of the sub-cloud, rotates it slightly one way or the other, then translates it into the right position.

The basic IFS algorithm is simple and short enough to state right here and now:

1. $x \leftarrow 0, y \leftarrow 0$
2. for $n \leftarrow 1$ to 20,000
          $Z \leftarrow$ random (A,B,C,D,E,F)
          $(x,y) \leftarrow Z(x,y)$
          if n $>$ 10 then plot (x,y)

On this basis, readers may construct the program I call CLOUD. In the first step, the variables x and y are set to 0. The second step involves a loop that repeats the basic iteration process 20,000 times. Readers are free to change this number if the images that result look either too dense or too light.

Within the loop, I have condensed what will ultimately be many program instructions into single lines. For example, the "instruction" $Z \leftarrow$ random (A,B,C,D,E,F) really means, "Choose one of the six transformations A, B, C, D, E, or F based on their relative probabilities of .21, .09, .22 and .27, .13 or .08." How is this done? Imagine a one-unit line segment that is subdivided into consecutive lengths equal to these probabilities. The first division point would lie at .21, the second at .30 and the third at .52 and so on. In each case, merely add the current probability to the ongoing sum.

If a random number between 0 and 1 is chosen, it must lie somewhere on the unit line. The segment that it happens to fall into will be the basis on which the program CLOUD chooses which transformation to apply next.

A simple algorithm for this process would involve six separate tests. I have displayed the first three below so that readers will get the general idea:

1. $r \leftarrow$ random
2. if $r < .21$ then transform A
3. if $r > = .21$ and $r < .30$ then transform B
4. if $r > = .30$ and $r < .52$ then transform C etc.

Even this algorithm is not quite complete. What, after all, do the commands "transform A," and so on, mean? The structure that I have chosen for CLOUD must expand each of these commands into little algorithms of their own, algorithms that correspond, in fact, to the second line of the loop.

To actually carry out transformation B, for example, requires two steps:

1. $x' \leftarrow .08x - .199y - 5.6$
2. $y' \leftarrow .199x + .08y - .04$

These instructions will look a little friendlier to readers who glance at the second line of the IFS table on page 122: The numbers .08, $- .199$, .199, .08, $- 5.6$ and $- 0.4$ appear in the second row, the one for transformation B.

Each of the four algorithmic modules "transform A," "transform B," and so on, must be translated into similar two-line algorithms, each followed by the assignments of x' and y' back into x and y.

In the final stage of the loop, the point (x, y) must be plotted. This is not quite as simple as saying, "plot (x,y)." Indeed, the programmer of CLOUD must use an appropriate screen coordinate system. Suppose that your display screen happens to be 200 pixels wide and 100 pixels high. The coordinate system used in the four transformations described places the origin in the middle of the cloud. But in most computer screens, the origin lies on the left side of the screen, either at the top or the bottom. How do you "plot" the point (x, y)?

The answer lies in using two systems of coordinates, one for computation of the cloud, the other for display purposes. The first system of coordinates is used for a virtual cloud, so to speak, that we never see. The second system of coordinates is used strictly for display purposes. Thus, every time a new point (x,y) in the virtual cloud is computed by the program, it must convert these coordinates into a new point (w,z) in the display cloud.

The virtual cloud happens to be 14 units (of graph paper) in diameter. To create a display cloud that is, say 112 pixels in diameter, the virtual coordinates must each be multiplied by 8. But that is not enough. They must also be translated from the left edge of the screen over to the middle. The following statements will handle the case of a 20- by-100 screen that has its origin in the upper left corner. The variables w and z represent the display coordinates.

1. $w \leftarrow 8x + 100$
2. $z \leftarrow 8y - 50$

This completes the description of CLOUD. I will not claim for a moment that I have selected the best possible collage for my cloud. Others may find a better arrangement of sub-clouds that fill the overall shape in a more natural or aesthetically exciting fashion. In general, the more open space within the collage that is not covered by sub-figures, the more open and diffuse the resulting graphic image will be.

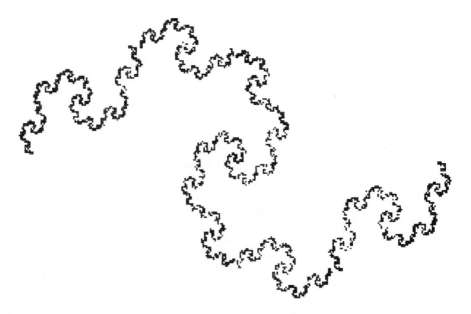

Figure 12.3 IFS-generated fractal wave.

The second IFS fractal represents the element water. This time I will
use not a two-dimensional collage but a one-dimensional one. Figure
12.4 shows a pair of spirals joined together at their apexes to produce a
shape that, overall, looks somewhat like a wave. The shape may be regarded as a one-dimensional "region" that may be sub-divided into
spheres of influence for three separate transformations, A, B, and C.

The first transformation, A, maps the entire double-spiral wave into
a smaller version of itself still centered on the apex. This transformation
not only shrinks, but it rotates the figure so that it still fits the smaller
portion of itself. The second transformation maps the entire wave into
the small wavelet labelled B in the figure. Readers will see at once that
this is simply a smaller version of the entire double spiral placed at the
trailing edge of the large wave.

But what about the other half of the wave, the trough into which it
threatens to crash with a fractal roar? The third transformation, C, simply rotates the entire figure by 180 degrees so that whatever gets generated on one side of the image has a chance of being mapped over to the
other side in order to complete the picture. In fact, because the right half
of the wave has half the area, the third transformation gets half the action. The probability with which the program I call WAVE uses transfor-

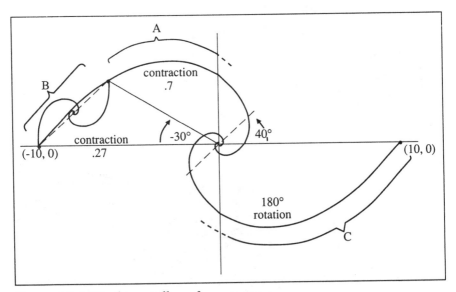

Figure 12.4 Working collage for a wave.

	a	b	c	d	e	f	p
A	.606	.35	−.35	.606	0	0	.35
B	.207	−.174	.174	.207	−7.9	1.6	.15
C	−1	0	0	−1	0	0	.50

mation C is exactly .5. The table above shows the IF system I developed to produce the wave image. Readers are free to write their own version of WAVE, using these equations or others they might wish to derive for themselves.

This raises the question, of course, "Just how do you find those equations?" Insofar as they involve only contractions, rotations, and translations, they can be calculated on the basis of measurements taken directly from the figure you have drawn on graph paper.

Consider, for example, the subcloud B in the cloud collage in Figure 12.2. Its diameter, as I measured it on squared paper, was 3 units while the cloud as a whole had a diameter of 14 units. This meant that the program would have to shrink the large cloud by a factor of $3/14$ or .214. Next, I decided that the small cloud should reproduce the whole cloud at an angle of 68 degrees in the positive sense. This would turn it well to the left so that the same surface would be reproduced in the cloudlet at the part where it seemingly emerged from the main cloud.

The formulas for a, b, c, and d are based on the theory of affine transformations which, luckily, needn't concern us here. As it happens, simple trigonometric functions do all the work:

$$a = .214\cos(68) \quad b = .214\sin(68)$$
$$c = .214\sin(68) \quad d = .214\cos(68)$$

In each case, the contraction factor is multiplied by the cosine or sine of the angle of rotation. If we calculate these numbers on a hand calculator, the first four numbers in row B of the cloud's IFS table emerge.

The translations, e and f, turn out to be especially easy to calculate. The shrunken and rotated sub-object has the same relation to the origin as the whole object does. Where does the origin go when the sub-object is at last translated to its final resting place? The horizontal distance is e and the vertical distance is f.

By now, some readers will be pondering some elementary creations of their own. How to make a mountain or fire? Should a two-dimensional or one-dimensional collage be used? The answer to the second question depends on whether the fractal appearance aimed at is essentially one- or two-dimensional. Take mountains, for example. I can imagine a mountain in outline as a series of sub-mountains that mount to the summit. I can also imagine it as a more or less solid object with a fractal outline.

As for fire, imagine a collage with a large flame composed of three subflames, two at the base of the flame and one at the top.

This much completes the excursion into the elements of IFS systems, not nature's workshop, but your own.

Further Reading

Michael F. Barnsley. *Fractals Everywhere.* Academic Press, 1988.
Benoit B. Mandelbrot. *The Fractal Geometry of Nature.* W. H. Freeman, 1983.

MATHEMATICS MATTERS

Mathematics, once described by the great popularizer, Eric Temple Bell, as "the queen and servant of the sciences," displays some tiny perfect gems from her crown jewels in the first chapter of this suite. The spheres of Dandelin provide a startling proof that points on an ellipse enjoy the equidistance property: the sums of their distances from the two foci of the ellipse are all equal! Other gems illustrate other proofs, laying bare the real motivation of those who become mathematicians. To know and appreciate the process of proof is to have the ear and speech of the queen herself, to hold a few of her crystalline secrets in your hand.

Golygon City and the art of cat-scanning illustrate the search for truth as most mathematicians experience it. Conjectures are made, then either proved or disproved. It astonishes most people, including mathematicians, that results that seem to apply only to some abstruse or toy system can suddenly turn out to have important, even life-saving applications. Cat scans turn this situation around by showing how image reconstruction gives rise to interesting mathematics even when there are only a handful of x-rays available.

A whole branch of mathematics, the theory of rigidity, addresses the problem of determining when an arbitrary structure of rods and joints is rigid and when it will flex. A bracing excursion into the problem of making cubic and rectangular frameworks rigid illustrates real problems faced by rigidity theorists and the theories they have discovered to solve those problems.

A book of this nature cannot stray long from the computational realm. Mathematical thinking has long been thought to comprise an important area of human IQ. Whether the term "intelligence quotient" has any definite meaning, IQ tests certainly abound with mathematical examples. Can an IQ test-writing program succeed? This one completes sequences and solves analogy problems with frightening success.

To end with a program that solves IQ test problems merely serves to introduce the next section, where computers enter the arts.

13

MATHEMATICAL MORSELS

Ross Honsberger has spent more than two decades collecting mathematical morsels for general consumption. Attending one of his rare public lectures, I had the pleasure of sampling one of his mathematical feasts. I found it not just palatable but downright delicious.

Honsberger, who teaches mathematics at the University of Waterloo in Canada, will stop at nothing to demonstrate mathematical principles. To illustrate a topological tidbit one day, he wandered into a colleague's lecture wearing his trousers inside out. He announced that he would turn them right side out without really taking them off.

To show that the trousers would not "really" be removed, he tied his own ankles together with an eight-foot length of rope. He proceeded to pull both trouser legs down onto the rope, revealing his favorite heart-spotted undershorts. The students watched closely for any deception as he first twisted the pants through the rope, then turned them right side out and finally wriggled back into them. I can testify that Honsberger's trick requires neither magic nor mirrors.

I listened to Honsberger's lecture near my hometown in Ontario. He served to the audience such delights as spheres in a cone, checkers on a board, dots on a dish and beans in a Greek urn.

Honsberger began by describing the marvelous spheres of Germinal Dandelin, a 19th-century Belgian mathematician. Dandelin discovered

131

an amazing connection between the classical and modern concepts of the ellipse. The Greeks conceived of an ellipse as the figure that results when a plane cuts obliquely through a cone. Since the time of Descartes, however, the ellipse has been described analytically in terms of two special points called foci. The sum of the distances from the two foci to any point on the ellipse is constant.

Honsberger introduced Dandelin's spheres by drawing our attention to a projected transparency of a plane cutting a cone. (Readers can follow Dandelin's argument with occasional glances at Figure 13.1.) I cannot swear that what follows are Honsberger's exact words, but he readily admits to a certain, broad similarity:

"It takes no genius to see that the plane divides the cone into two pieces. But it was Dandelin's idea to insert a sphere into each piece. Like an over-inflated balloon, each sphere contacts the wall of the cone and touches the elliptical plane at a certain point. But where? One can imagine Dandelin's heart leaping at the thought that the two spheres might touch the plane at the two focal points of the ellipse."

Honsberger places his marking pen on the transparency. He labels the two points of contact by the symbols F and G. Are these the foci of the ellipse?

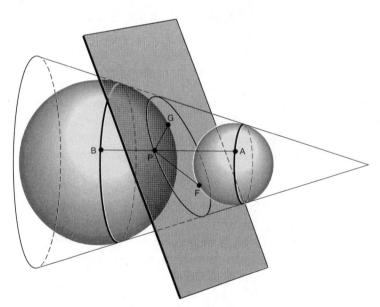

Figure 13.1 An ellipse in a cone separates Dandelin's spheres.

"Let's take a look at what clever old Dandelin did. First, through any point P that we care to select on the ellipse, we may draw a straight line that runs up the side of the cone to its tip. Second, the line will touch the two spheres at two points, say, A and B. No matter where we pick P to lie on the ellipse, the length of AB will be the same.

"Ah, but that gives it away! The distance from the point F to P equals the distance from P to A. After all, both PF and PA are tangents to the same sphere from the same point. By the same reasoning, the distance from the second point, G, to P equals the distance from B to P. Are we not finished? $PF + PG = PA + PB$, and the latter sum is just the (constant) length of AB.

"Now isn't that the darndest thing?" Honsberger sounds rural.

As I look around the lecture hall, students appear stunned. Professors alternately smile and frown. One of them behind me murmurs, "Well, I'll be."

Without pausing for a breath, Honsberger serves up the next morsel. We find ourselves staring at a slide of a peculiar board game.

"Here's a simple little exercise in checker-jumping. I imagine that such a clever audience will have no trouble figuring this one out." A devilish gleam invades his eye, a warning that something unusual is about to happen.

The slide shows a grid of squares with a line drawn through it (see Figure 13.2). Honsberger explains the rules: solvers can arrange a given number of checkers any way they like behind the line. Checkers can be jumped and removed in the vertical or horizontal direction, but the final jump can leave only one checker. The problem is to decide how many checkers it will take, at a minimum, to "propel" the last checker a given distance d beyond the line. In deciding this, solvers must also devise an arrangement that allows the frenzy of jumping to take place.

"Does anybody want to take a crack at this problem?" Honsberger looks up at the audience, sees there are no takers and smiles ingenuously.

"Well, then, let's try a few examples."

He places two checkers adjacent to each other on the board, jumps the back checker over the front one, then strides triumphantly to the blackboard, where he writes

d	number of checkers
1	2

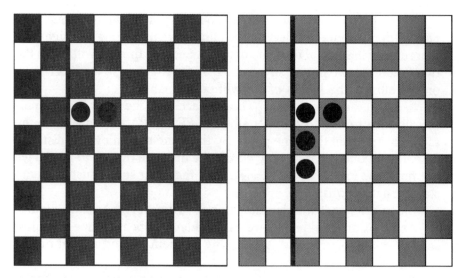

Figure 13.2 Four checker-jumping arrangements.

Next he places four checkers on the board. He jumps the checkers until a single checker is left in the second row.

"I'm just saving you people the trouble of figuring it out. Believe me, this is the best that anyone can do." He writes "2" under "*d*" and "4" under "number of checkers." He creates another configuration of eight checkers and manages to propel one checker to the third row. He scribbles "3" and "8" on the blackboard.

"Anybody want to guess how many checkers it takes to send one checker four units beyond the line?"

Somebody volunteers the figure 16. No. The answer turns out to be 20 checkers, at a minimum.

The audience is now getting somewhat worked up. Could the relation between distance and the number of checkers be described by one of those superexponential functions? Perhaps it will take a million checkers to send one checker five units beyond the line. When Honsberger reveals the answer, members of the audience look at one another, smiling uncomfortably.

"Alas! A million checkers will not be enough, nor a billion. It is simply impossible, no matter how many checkers you assemble behind the line or how you arrange them. It was John Conway, the Cambridge mathematician, who proved the task impossible."

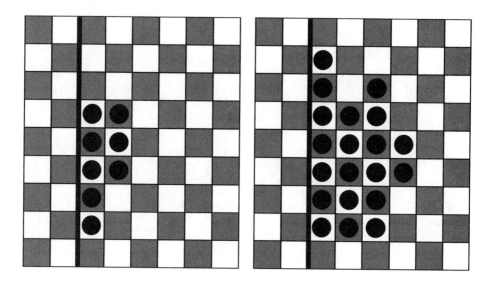

Honsberger does not stop the lecture to describe Conway's difficult proof, although he would not dream of discouraging anyone from attempting it. Instead he quickly moves on to a discussion of the pigeonhole principle.

This famed principle simply states that if I build 9,999 pigeonholes for 10,000 pigeons, at least one of the holes would house more than one bird. The pigeonhole principle has been used to prove many theorems in combinatorics, the branch of mathematics that deals with finite collections.

"The next mathematical morsel is one of the strangest applications of the pigeonhole principle ever made. Imagine that someone has placed 650 points inside a circle of radius 16 units. You have been given an annulus, a flat ring in the shape of a washer. The outside radius of the washer is three units, and the inside radius is two. You are then challenged to place the washer so that it covers at least 10 of the 650 points."

"Impossible," whispers an impetuous undergraduate behind me. "What if all the points are in a tiny area?"

"Then he can cover all of them with one washer, you *idiot*!" retorts another student.

Is it really possible to cover 10 points with the washer? Honsberger begins the proof by drawing a diagram shown in Figure 13.3. He invites

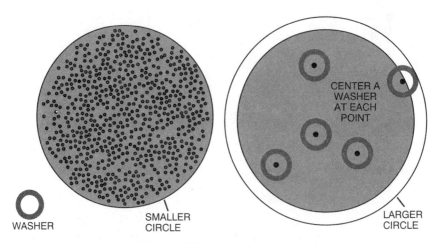

Figure 13.3 The washer problem.

us to imagine that a copy of the washer has been centered at each of the 650 points inside the circle.

Some of the points may be near the edge of the circle, in which case some of the annuli will extend beyond its circumference. But because each point lies inside the circle and because the washer has radius three, all the annuli will lie within the larger circle having the same center and having radius 19, that is, the sum of 16 and three. The area of the washer is the difference between the area of a circle of radius three and one of radius two. This comes to five times π.

"The 650 washers blanket the large circle with a total coverage of 650 times 5π, that is $3{,}250\pi$. Of course, much of the coverage will be overlapping, but suppose for the moment that no point of the inner circle is buried under more than nine washers. In such a case, the total amount of area covered within the larger circle could not come to more than $3{,}249\pi$, nine times the area of the circle. But because $3{,}249\pi$ is less than $3{,}250\pi$, some point, x, must be covered by at least 10 washers. The pigeonhole principle strikes again."

Honsberger pauses to catch his breath. "You see it now, don't you?" Then he feigns surprise. "You don't?"

The application of the pigeonhole principle is clear enough, but some of us are confused. We thought the idea was to cover 10 points by one washer, not to hide some point x under 10 washers. Suddenly, our minds are turned inside out like a pair of trousers.

"Look at the point x. If you take away the 10 washers that cover it and replace these by a single washer centered at x, then that washer alone must cover the centers of the 10 washers that we took away. Each of these centers is one of the 650 original points!" The morsel is digested as we hear a faint gulp from somewhere at the back of the lecture room.

The pièce de résistance of Honsberger's menu arrives in the form of a Grecian urn adorning his next transparency (see Figure 13.4). "How much can a Grecian earn?" quips Honsberger.

When the groans have died away, he explains the problem. An urn is filled with 75 white beans and 150 black ones. Next to the urn is a large pile of black beans. The beans are removed from the urn according to certain rules.

Figure 13.4 What is the color of the last of 75 white beans and 150 black ones in the urn?

"Here's how it works. Remove two beans from the urn at random. If at least one of the two beans is black, place it on the pile and drop the other bean, whether white or black, back into the urn. But if both of the removed beans are white, discard both of them and take one black bean from the pile and drop it into the urn."

"Each time a Greek or anyone else dips into the urn to remove two beans at random, either operation ensures that there will be one fewer bean in the urn that there was before the move. Slowly and steadily, the original supply of black and white beans dwindles. At last there are three beans left in the urn, then two, then one. What color is the last bean?"

The simple and startling answer is white. By figuring out why, a Greek can earn intangible delights worth more than a hill of beans.

Further Reading

Ross Honsberger, ed. *Mathematical Gems: From Elementary Combinatorics, Number Theory, and Geometry*. Dolciani Mathematical Expositions, No. 1. Mathematical Association of America, 1973.

Ross Honsberger, ed. *Mathematical Morsels*. Dolciani Mathematical Expositions, No. 3. Mathematical Association of America, 1979.

Ross Honsberger, ed. *Mathematical Plums*. Dolciani Mathematical Expositions, No. 4. Mathematical Association of America, 1979.

14

GOLYGON CITY

A journey of a thousand miles must begin with a
single step.

LAO-TZU, *The Way of Lao-tzu*

Allow me to start you on a journey in Golygon City. You can take a similar trip in New York, Kyoto, or almost any large city whose streets form a grid of squares. Here are your directions. Stroll down a city block, and at the end turn left or right. Walk two more blocks, turn left or right, then walk another three blocks, turn once more and so on. Each time you turn, you must walk straight one block farther than you did before. If after a number of turns you arrive at your starting point, you have traced a golygon. If you do not need the physical exercise, you can easily simulate the journey by moving a pencil along a piece of graph paper with a square grid. If you become lost, you may refer to Figure 14.1.

A golygon consists of straight-line segments that have lengths (measured in miles, meters, or whatever unit you prefer) of one, two, three and so on, up to some finite number. Every segment connects at a right angle to the segment that is one unit larger—except the longest segment, which meets the shortest segment at a right angle. Golygons are more than just a geometric curiosity. They have inspired some delightful puzzles as well as some intriguing problems for research. What better way to develop insight into the research process than to take a recreational journey?

It seems that golygons were first conceived by Lee Sallows, a redoubtable engineer of the Catholic University Nijmegen in the Netherlands. I first featured Sallow's work in *The Armchair Universe* (see Further Reading) where I described his search for pangrams, sentences

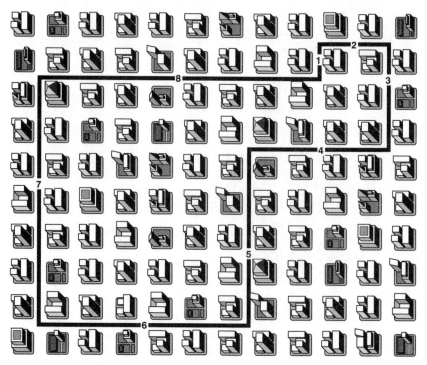

Figure 14.1 A map of Golygon City.

containing each letter of the alphabet. Since then Sallows has invented many new recreations but none so engaging as golygons.

In the fall of 1988 Sallows began his search for golygons. It did not take him long to find an eight-sided golygon. Yet he could find no such objects that had fewer than eight sides. Nor did he discover a golygon with nine sides, nor 10, nor 11, . . . until at last he stumbled on a 16-sided golygon.

Wondering whether he had missed any, Sallows wrote a computer program to automate the search. It spewed out no less than 28 different 16-sided golygons (see Figure 14.2) before moving on to higher orders. The program did not find golygons with from 17 up to 23 sides, but it generated numerous 24-sided golygons — 2,108 to be exact.

By then Sallows had a hunch that the number of sides in a golygon must be a multiple of eight. Yet his program, which was already laboring in the 20's, was unequal to the task of discovering any 32-sided golygons. Frustrated, Sallows appealed to Martin Gardner, the supreme au-

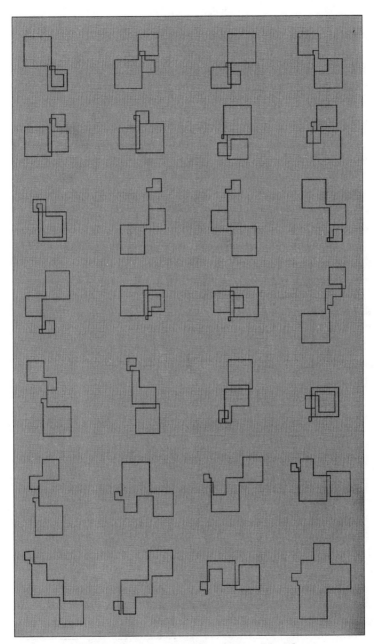

Figure 14.2 All 28 golygons that have 16 sides.

thority in matters of recreational mathematics. Could Gardner prove that the number of sides in a golygon must be a multiple of eight?

We can creep up on Gardner's proof by starting with the simpler task of proving that the number of sides must be a multiple of two. To explain, allow me to take you back to Golygon City. We start our journey by walking one block to the north. (I choose north only for convenience.) Hence, the first side of the golygon will run north for one block. Next we can turn either left or right, that is, west or east. Therefore, the second side of the golygon will run either two blocks to the west or two blocks to the east. It follows that all odd sides in the golygon (the first, third, fifth, etc.) are an odd number of blocks long and run north or south; all even sides (the second, fourth, sixth, etc.) are an even number of blocks long and run east or west. Because the last side of the golygon meets the first at right angles, the last side must run east or west. Therefore, the last block is an even side of the golygon, and the number of sides in a golygon must be a multiple of two.

To show that the number of sides must be a multiple of four, we begin by calculating the total distance we traveled to the north of the starting point. To do this, we simply add the number of blocks we walked to the north and subtract the number of blocks we traveled to the south. (A net negative distance to the north simply means that we are south of the starting point.)

Because all north and south sides are an odd number of blocks long, we are essentially adding and subtracting consecutive odd numbers. It takes only a little tinkering to convince ourselves that the result is always even when we add or subtract an even number of odd lengths — for example, $1 + 3 - 5 + 7 = 6$. By the same token, an odd number of odd lengths always gives an odd sum. Therefore, the distance walked north is an even number of blocks if and only if we have walked along an even number of north and south sides.

Now if we walk from the starting point around Golygon City and return, the distance to the north of the starting point equals zero. Because zero is an even number, the golygon must have an even number of north and south sides. The total number of sides is twice the number of north and south sides, because for every north or south side there must be an east or west side. Therefore, the number of sides in a golygon is a multiple of four.

How on earth did Gardner show that the number of sides must be a multiple of eight? Let us accompany the master of his journey.

The horizontal sides of a golygon may be divided up into an east set and a west set. The sums of numbers in each set are even and equal. Suppose for a moment that a golygon has n sides, where n is a multiple of 4 but not 8. If you add up the horizontal legs in such a golygon, you will obtain a number in the sequence 6, 42, 110, 210, 342. But then either the sum of east sides or the sum of west sides (it doesn't matter which) will turn out to be a number in the sequence 3, 21, 55, 105, 171, and so on. All of these numbers are odd, contradicting the fact that the sums of the east and west sides are both even. The only way to get out of this difficulty is to realize that n must be a multiple of 8.

Gardner's proof may seem rather peculiar because even numbers played a major role and odd numbers hardly entered into the discussion. The same conclusion can be reached, however, by making a similar argument on behalf of the odd lengths. In fact, the two kinds of lengths play independent roles in the construction of any golygon. One may obtain, for example, a new golygon from two others of the same size by using the even lengths from the first golygon and the odd lengths from the second.

Our recreational path has so far taken us from the question of existence to the question of conditions on that existence; the number of sides in a golygon must definitely be a multiple of eight. For convenience I will call this theorem the $8k$ condition for two-dimensional golygons. It is what mathematicians call a necessary condition. If a golygon exists, the number of its sides is necessarily a multiple of eight. But is this condition sufficient? In other words, if we merely ask that the number of sides, n, be a multiple of eight, is that sufficient to guarantee the existence of a golygon?

We can find a golygon that has eight times any number of sides by applying a set of simple instructions. The first step is to decide how large a value of n one wants. To illustrate the method, I will choose a 16-sided golygon. The second step is to write down consecutive numbers from 1 to n, in this case, from 1 to 16.

The third step would have us place plus and minus signs in front of the numbers. The first quarter and the last quarter of the numbers will receive plus signs, and all the numbers in between will receive minus signs:

$$+ 1, \ + 2, \ + 3, \ + 4, \ - 5, \ - 6, \ - 7, \ - 8, \ - 9,$$
$$- 10, \ - 11, \ - 12, \ + 13, \ + 14, \ + 15, \ + 16.$$

To translate this sequence of numbers into a tour of Golygon City, you need only know that positive odd numbers run to the north, negative odd numbers to the south, positive even numbers to the east and negative even numbers to the west. The golygon that corresponds to these numbers looks like a snake. A 32-sided "snake" is shown in Figure 14.3.

Having settled the question of sufficiency of the $8k$ condition, Gardner and Sallows began to wonder just how many golygons should exist. They had found one of order eight, 28 of order 16 and 2,108 of order 24. How many would there be of higher orders? Such questions are most frequently asked by mathematicians who specialize in combinatorics, the study of discrete mathematical objects such as sets and graphs. Gardner decided to check with some experts. He wrote letters to computer scientist Donald E. Knuth of Stanford University and to mathematician Richard K. Guy of the University of Calgary in Alberta. Could either of them assist in the matter of enumerating golygons?

Before long, Knuth had written a computer program that counted all the golygons up to 64 sides. The total number of 64-sided golygons, for instance, is 127,674,038,970,623. Unfortunately, Knuth's program became unwieldy at larger sizes.

Meanwhile Guy was able to develop a formula that expressed the approximate number of golygons for each possible value of k, where k equals the number of sides divided by eight. The formula consists of a fraction, the principal parts of which are 2 raised to the power $8k - 6$ in the numerator and k cubed in the denominator. Because, as k increases, the exponential term increases much more rapidly than the cubed term, the growth and the number of golygons is basically exponential. Guy's formula has the further important property of being asymptotic, that is, it gives a value that, expressed as a percentage of the true value, comes increasingly close to 100 percent as k gets larger and larger.

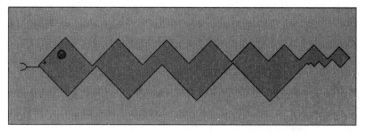

Figure 14.3 One golygon snake that has 32 sides.

Sallows, Gardner, Knuth, and Guy decided to report their various results in a paper. The word "golygon" does not appear in the title. Instead it is called "Serial Isogons of 90 Degrees," a name that rings more solemnly in the halls of mathematics than "golygons." The reference to 90 degrees implies that other kinds of golygons might be assembled. Indeed, some of the authors have looked at golygons in which every angle is not 90 degrees but 60 or 120 degrees. To construct such golygons, readers may need hexagonal-grid paper, which can be found in most graphics-supply stores.

Would this have been a good place to stop? Research (like recreation) never stops. Often, as research in one question progresses, other questions suggest themselves. Sometimes it is very hard to decide just what question to work on.

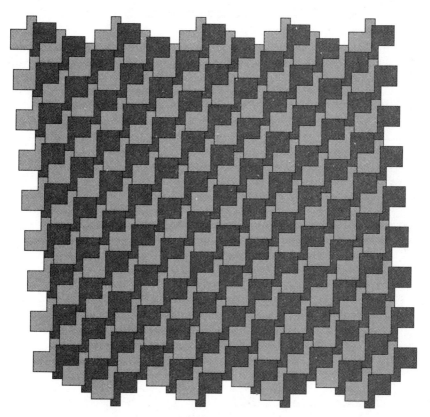

Figure 14.4 The smallest golygon tiles the plane.

Research problems are no sooner solved than the recreationist in us thinks of new avenues of inquiry: Can we find prime-sided golygons? The lengths of consecutive sides here increase by the sequence of odd primes: 1, 3, 5, 7, 11, 13 and so on.

Another offshoot of golygons deserves mention. Readers are urged to look at the eight-sided golygon once again. It is unique, the only member of its class. Eight-sided golygons will fit together very nicely to make tiling patterns. They will, as the professionals say, "tile the plane." Figure 14.4 shows an attractive tiling.

Properly speaking, the region bounded by an eight-sided golygon should be called a polyomino. Not all golygons produce polyominoes because some golygons intersect themselves in their meandering march around the plane. In fact, polyominid golygons (a formidable expression by which readers can lose friends and influence people) are probably increasingly rare in relative terms as *n* gets large. Only four of the 28 golygons shown in Figure 14.2 are the boundaries of polyominoes. None of these appears to tile the plane.

But in the matter of tiling, Sallows has a challenge for readers: suppose the eight-sided golygon represents the boundary of one's kitchen floor. Given 13 L-shaped tiles, can readers cover the kitchen floor exactly with these eccentric tiles? For the purpose of this question, the

Figure 14.5 A logolygon crated by Sallow.

floor may be thought of as divided into 52 squares, like the squares of the special paper on which this enquiry started. Each square is one step on a side. The L-shaped tiles consist of three squares in a row and an additional square comprising the foot of the L. Anyone who finds the task impossible must, of course, prove it to be so.

I close with some final words from Sallows, the engineer who started all this. The "words" are ZERO, ONE, TWO and so on, up to FIFTEEN. They can be arranged in a special golygon all their own in which the letters of these words determine the sides of what can only be called a logolygon (see Figure 14.5).

Further Reading

A. K. Dewdney. *The Armchair Universe: An Exploration of Computer Worlds.* W. H. Freeman, 1987.

Lee Sallows, Martin Gardner, Richard Guy, and Donald Knuth. "Serial Isogons of 90 Degrees." *Mathematics Magazine*, Vol. 64, No. 5 (Dec. 1991), pp. 315–324.

15

SCANNING THE CAT

This time (the Cheshire Cat) vanished quite slowly,
beginning with the end of the tail, and ending with
the grin, which remained some time after the rest of
it had gone.

LEWIS CARROLL, *Alice's Adventures in Wonderland*

The medical practice called CAT scanning herein lends its name to a new recreation in which readers attempt to reconstruct unknown objects on the basis of what might be called digital X rays, or D rays. A Cheshire cat may not be reconstructible from its grin, but some cats can be reconstructed from their D rays.

In 1979 Allan M. Cormack and Sir Godfrey N. Hounsfield shared the Nobel prize in medicine for the invention of the CAT scanner. Short for computed axial tomography, the machine combines a computer and a series of X-ray "slices" of a patient to reconstruct a cross section of his or her anatomy, replete with bones, vessels, fat, and other tissues.

An ordinary X-ray machine creates a two-dimensional image that is akin to a shadow. In sunlight, my shadow on the wall shows clearly an outline of my body. But in the "light" of an X-ray beam, my outline is filled in by bones and other internal organs. CAT scans are not like this at all. Here the X rays do not spray everywhere through my body. Instead they are confined to a single plane. On the other side of my body they produce what can only be called a one-dimensional shadow, a strip of dark and light that betrays the presence of bones and organs only within that plane and only as seen from that angle.

As shown in Figure 15.1, a medical technician positions a patient inside a CAT scanner so that an X-ray source may project its beam through the patient within a specific plane. On the other side of the patient a row

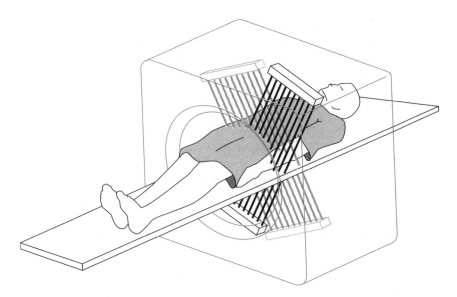

Figure 15.1 A patient inside a CAT scanner.

of detectors records the radiation that went through the patient along that particular angle. From here, the one-dimensional shadow is relayed in digital form to a computer. All of this conspires to make but one snapshot, so to speak.

The next snapshot is taken from a slightly different angle. The X-ray detector and source are rotated a bit, and a new beam of X rays slices through the patient within the same plane. The new array of readings is also sent to the computer.

When enough snapshots have been taken, the computer begins to reconstruct the patient's cross section in the plane of all the X rays. How is this done? It hardly takes a Nobel laureate to understand it. In fact, we shall do precisely the same kind of thing as the computer on a humbler scale. Rather than asking readers to spend half a million dollars on a CAT scanner, I shall provide some recreational CAT scanning that requires nothing more than pencil and graph paper.

The recreational version I call simply the catscanner reconstructs two-dimensional images composed of small black-and-white squares in an image grid as in Figure 15.2. For those who see no challenge in this exercise, let me hasten to add that the image is normally not provided, only the information from the so-called D rays.

The image is traversed, from two directions only, by D rays. A beam of horizontal D rays penetrates the object from right to left and is recorded as a sequence of numbers. Each number is the sum of the black squares in a particular row of the image grid. A beam of vertical D rays streams through the object from bottom to top. The beam is also recorded as a sequence of numbers with the same interpretation, namely, the number of black squares, one number per column. In Figure 15.2, for example, the number beside the second row is 2 because the second row contains two black squares. Each black square adds one to each number. From such a simple observation springs an important fact for catscanners: the sum of the row readings equals the sum of the column readings.

Theoretical niceties aside, can the image be reconstructed from just two beams? The answer depends on the particular pattern of black-and-white squares that makes up the object. For convenience, I will describe those patterns that we may logically reconstruct as "categorical" and those that cannot be constructed as "catastrophic."

Before I get too involved in what characterizes a catastrophic pattern, I offer an example that will prove to be categorical. The example is the spiral shown in Figure 15.2. After the catscanner has bombarded the spiral pattern with D rays, the sensors next to the rows reveal the sequence 8, 2, 6, 4, 5, 3, 7, whereas the sensors over the columns read 7, 1, 6, 3, 4, 5, 2, 7.

To reproduce the spiral from the two sequences, the catscanner could generate every combination of black-and-white squares until it found a pattern that would produce the original sequences. Luckily, we can develop a better technique to reconstruct the spiral.

In any set of sensor readings derived from a categorical pattern, one of the readings in one of the sequences will always match the number of nonzero readings in the other sequence. For the spiral pattern, the sensors next to the rows indicate seven nonzero readings, and the sequence associated with the first column contains a "7." It can therefore be deduced that the first column contains seven black squares in all seven rows.

These seven black squares contribute one unit to each of the readings associated with the rows. To determine the positions of other black squares, therefore, you change the 7 to a 0 in the column sequence and subtract one from each nonzero reading in the row sequence. Two new sequences result:

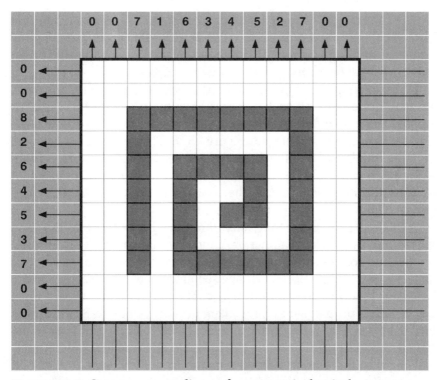

Figure 15.2 Catscanner readings of a categorical spiral.

Rows: 7, 1, 5, 3, 4, 2, 6
Columns: 0, 1, 6, 3, 4, 5, 2, 7

Notice that at least one reading in one of the sequences is equal to the number of the nonzero readings in the other sequence. In fact, because there are more than one, readers may take their pick of which one to work on next. The final outcome will be the same. If, for example, you pick the 7 in the first sequence, fill in the appropriate squares and carry out the arithmetic, the next sequence is:

Rows: 0, 1, 5, 3, 4, 2, 6
Columns: 0, 0, 5, 2, 3, 4, 1, 6

Once all the numbers have been reduced to zero, the picture of the spiral will be staring you in the face.

The catscanner does not decipher all patterns as easily as it does the spiral. A catastrophe would occur if two patterns that produced the same sequences of numbers were placed in the catscanner. By trial and error, you can probably come up with a few examples.

If you examine catastrophic patterns in a systematic way, however, you may notice that all such patterns have features that I call chains. Suppose that two different patterns — call then A and B — produce the same sequences of numbers (see Figure 15.3). Then pattern A must have the same number of rows and columns as pattern B. If pattern A is superposed on pattern B, there must be at least one black square in A that overlaps a white square in B. (Otherwise the patterns would not be different.) This square is the first link in the chain.

If this one square were the only difference between patterns A and B, however, the sensor readings of A and B would not agree. Therefore, the row that contains the first square must also include a second square that is white in A and black in B. The second square is the second link in the chain. Likewise the column that contains the second square must also include a third square that is black in A and white in B. This is the third link. A similar procedure can be repeated to find other links in the chain. Ultimately, the chain must be linked back to the first square, guaranteeing that there are no disagreements in the readings of A and B.

A study of catastrophic patterns leads to two theorems. The first states that a catastrophic pattern can be transformed into another by changing the color of each square in its chain. Such a transformation might be useful to describe ambiguous reconstructions. Indeed, the simple technique for reconstructing categorical patterns can be modified to partially reproduce catastrophic patterns. I invite readers to attempt this modification.

The second theorem says that a pattern is categorical if, and only if, it has no chains. Using the theorem, I wonder how many readers can now justify the method I gave earlier for reconstructing categorical patterns. How can I always be so confident of finding a number in one of the sequences that counts the nonzero numbers in the other sequence? A hint shall suffice: What would be the consequence for the pattern if no such numbers existed?

The second theorem can also be applied to determine the number of categorical patterns of a given size. For instance, although 512 patterns can be created by coloring the squares of a three-by-three grid, only 99 of them are categorical. The three-by-three categorical patterns are

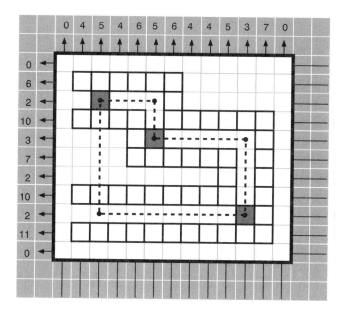

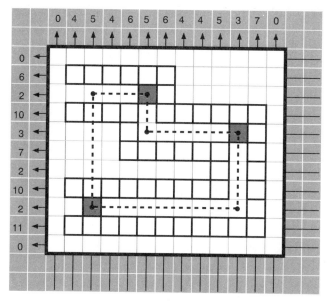

Figure 15.3 Patterns A and B and a chain that converts one into another.

shown in Figure 15.4. To save space, I have omitted those patterns that are reflections or rotations of others.

Readers who have access to computers can write a simple program that simulates the catscanner. The program I call GRIN (Figure 15.5) then stores the readings in two arrays that I cannot refrain from calling *x-array* and *y-array*. Next the program requests the number of non-zero entries in the two arrays and stores them in *xcount* and *ycount*.

GRIN searches through the arrays of catscanner readings until it finds the number *xcount* in the *y-array* or the number *ycount* in the *x-array*. The program carries out the appropriate arithmetic, draws the corresponding squares on the screen and then sets a special variable called *done* to 1. The last step prevents the program from repeating the previous instructions until it has had a chance to recompute *xcount* and *ycount*. When *xcount* reaches 0, the non-zero numbers have all been processed, *done* is set to 0 and the computer takes a catnap. A somewhat abbreviated version of the algorithm is given above.

Here are some categorical patterns to try out on your catscanner. Blending the medical with the recreational for a moment, the following categorical pattern was recently found in a CAT scan of a cat. What had it eaten?

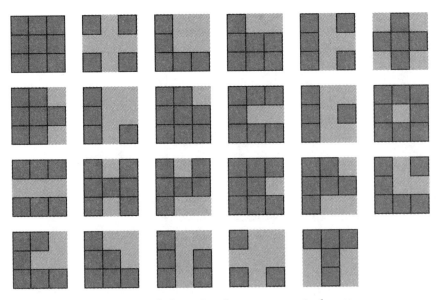

Figure 15.4 A census of three-by-three categorical patterns.

```
input x-array and y-array
input xcount and ycount
repeat
    done ← 0
    for each array position I
        if x-array (I) = ycount and done = 0
        then x-array (I) ← 0
                for each y-array (J) > 0
                        decrement y-array (J)
                        color square at (I,J)
                done ← 1
        if y-array (I) = xcount and done = 0
        then y-array (I) ← 0
                for each x-array (J) > 0
                        decrement x-array (J)
                        color square at (J,I)
                done ← 1
    compute new xcount and ycount
until xcount = 0
```

Figure 15.5 Outline for the GRIN program.

Rows: 9, 5, 7, 5, 6
Columns: 5, 3, 5, 0, 5, 2, 5, 0, 1, 5, 1

Recently someone brought me a box that he could not open, having lost the key. Could I determine the contents of the box? A catscanner revealed an object with an ambiguous reconstruction, but I immediately knew what it was.

Rows: 11, 5, 4
Columns: 3, 2, 3, 1, 1, 1, 1, 2, 3, 2, 1

Finally, here is the grand catscanning challenge of all. The use of square grids would appear to limit the reconstruction game to just two sets of D rays, one horizontal and the other vertical. But what about diagonals? If diagonal D rays are permitted, four sets of D rays are possible, and the class of objects that can be reliably reproduced is dramatically increased.

The following D rays were taken first horizontally, then diagonally, then vertically, then diagonally again.

Horizontal: 1, 13, 17, 17, **14**, 14, 12, 6, 6, 6
First diagonal: 1, 2, 5, 6, 4, 4, 6, 7, 7, 8, **8**, 5, 6, 6, 6, 6, 5, 5, 3, 3, 1, 1, 1
Vertical: 2, 1, 1, 3, 3, 6, 6, 8, 9, 7, 5, **5**, 5, 5, 6, 8, 8, 8, 4, 4, 2
Second diagonal: 1, 2, 2, 2, 2, 4, 5, 4, 5, 5, 4, 5, 6, **6**, 9, 9, 7, 5, 5, 4, 2, 3, 3, 3, 2, 1

The horizontal was recorded on the left of the object, the first diagonal beam was recorded on the lower left, the vertical beam was recorded below and the second diagonal beam was recorded below and to the right of the object. In each sequence, one of the numbers appears in bold type. This number represents the ray that passed through the center of the object.

The reconstruction process may use any insights contained herein, but there is no substitute for good old-fashioned logical thought. Readers may even try one of the first reconstruction techniques employed in medical imaging, the back-projection technique.

You can determine a minimal outline by drawing the region in which all four D rays are present over the grid. Then back-project: because each number corresponds to a specific ray (either horizontal, vertical, or diagonal), one can distribute the number back over every square in the ray as though it encountered a uniform shade of gray. That shade is captured by an average: divide the number of the ray by the number of squares in it.

The shade of gray can be entered in the squares numerically (but one must have a steady hand) or, better still, can be reflected by a number of dots. If the quotient turns out to be .8, for example, place eight dots in each of the squares of the ray. A quotient of 1.2 would then require 12 dots. The process is time-consuming but perfect for that long flight, quiet lunch, or slow evening. When a square is dotted in for a second, third, or even fourth time, room must be found for additional dots. At the end of the process, the object will be plainly visible, if not precisely rendered. It can be cleaned up by erasing all those squares that contain fewer than a certain number of points. This practice is known as thresholding.

To speed up the task, some readers might be able to adapt the GRIN program. Logicians will of course insist on deducing which squares are dark. This can be done by a process of elimination like the technique for reconstructing categorical patterns. Yet I think that logicians and programmers alike will find the solution to be the cat's meow.

Further Reading

Gabor T. Herman. *Image Reconstruction from Projections: The Fundamentals of Computerized Tomography.* Academic Press, 1980.

16

RIGID THINKING

London Bridge is broken down
My fair lady.

ANONYMOUS

It helps to be flexible when you think about rigidity. I learned this lesson in the summer of 1978 as my father, my son, Jonathan, and I fixed up our cabin in the Canadian North. To patch the leaky roof, my father had built a scaffold from freshly cut spruce poles. When my father and Jonathan climbed to the top of the scaffold, the rustic framework groaned and swayed. I mentioned that the scaffold looked a little shaky, but my father scoffed, "Why this thing will hold 10 men—and I used the absolute minimum number of poles."

Who was I to argue with my father, an expert woodsman and an amateur mathematician to boot? I returned to my chores inside the cabin. Less than a minute later I heard a whoosh, a thump and two startled cries. Racing outside, I found Jonathan and my father sprawled on the moss. The scaffolding had scaf-*folded*, so to speak. The two stood up, and my father grinned sheepishly, exclaiming, "Isn't that the damnedest thing!"

I can hardly blame my father for building an unstable scaffold. Mathematicians and engineers have been struggling for centuries with the theory and practice of constructing rigid frameworks. Mathematicians call the subject rigidity theory. I investigated this topic, hoping that a few insights might save my family and others from further injury. My research has also uncovered a host of amusing puzzles to flex the mind.

Rigidity theorists prefer not to make frameworks out of spruce poles and nails. Instead they have a mental construction set that consists of abstract bars that cannot be stretched, compressed, or bent by any amount of force. Such bars come in all conceivable lengths, and if the ends of two or more of them touch, an instant universal joint is formed. The joint allows the two bars to swivel and twist unless other connecting bars constrain their motion.

Imagine, for example, a framework of 12 bars of equal lengths arranged into a cube. The cubic framework is not rigid. Placed on a table, it would flop over in an instant. Indeed, if such a framework were rigid, bridges and towers would not need diagonal girders.

Recently I attempted to brace a cube by adding diagonal bars to some of its six square faces. How many bars would it take to make the cube rigid? Four bars, judiciously placed, seemed enough until I found a way to make the cube flex. Even a cube that had diagonal bars added to five of its faces turned out not to be rigid (Figure 16.1). The five bars, along with six of those already present in the cube, form two tetrahedrons that are hinged along a common bar. If the two tetrahedrons are folded against each other, two of the four joints that define the unbraced square face move toward each other as in Figure 16.1. The other two joints move outward. No matter how five diagonal bars are added to the faces of a cube, there will always be a way to flex it. No fewer than six bars are needed.

Instead of bracing a cube on its faces, what if it were braced by diagonal bars that run from one joint right through the center of the cube to the opposite joint? (With the careless élan of theorists, readers may ignore the intersections of the diagonals.) A cube braced by four interior diagonals has a strange kind of flexibility that theorists call an infinitesimal flex. In some sense, an infinitesimal flex is a motion of one part of a framework relative to another. The motion is so small, however, that it does not even exist.

Figure 16.1 The braced cube at the left has an ordinary flex (*center*), whereas the one at the right has an infinitesimal flex.

Let me explain. The diagonally braced cube shown in Figure 16.1 below has arrows that indicate a tiny rotation of the top face in relation to the bottom face. Because all bars making up the cube are made of ideal materials that will not suffer the slightest change in their length, the top face cannot be truly rotated, even by a tiny amount. Yet one may *start* to rotate the top face and the bottom face in opposite directions. During this vanishingly tiny moment, there is no resistance from any other part of the cube because all bars that connect the upper face to the lower one make right angles with the direction of rotation.

If this diagonally braced cube were made of real materials, it would be distinctly vulnerable to small but measurable rotations. The structure would wobble. (My father avoided this particular style of bracing.) Frameworks that have only infinitesimal flexes are considered rigid, but those that have no flexibility whatsoever are called infinitesimally rigid.

Besides their mental construction sets, rigidity theorists also have a mental tool kit containing a great many theorems and techniques that can be applied, among other things, to bracing a cube. One of the simplest and most effective tools was discovered by 19th-century engineers. A framework that has J joints must have at least $3J - 6$ bars to be infinitesimally rigid. This theorem can be applied to the cube; its eight joints mean that $J = 8$. The corresponding magic number computed by the formula is $(3 \times 8) - 6 = 18$.

To show that a cube composed of 18 bars (12 edges and six braces) is actually infinitesimally rigid, one might appeal to a theorem discovered by the Russian geometer A. D. Alexandrov in the 1940s. Alexandrov studied rigidity in frameworks based on a convex polyhedron. These faceted surfaces include everything from cubes to cut gems to the geodesic domes of R. Buckminster Fuller. Alexandrov proved that any framework based on one of these shapes can be made infinitesimally rigid by adding bars to the framework so that every face is composed of triangles. As far as Alexandrov's theorem is concerned, then, a triangular bracing of each face of the cube (one bar each) will make it strong.

I sympathize with any readers who have problems visualizing the cubic bracings. Even the diagrams in Figure 16.1 are a bit complicated. Perhaps it is time to descend from the three-dimensional space that gave birth to the theory down to the plane, a two-dimensional space inhabited by a vast panoply of various flat frameworks. Although readers can easily figure out that a square can be made rigid with a single diagonal, they will find it rather challenging to figure out how to brace a grid of squares. For example, how many diagonals must be added to make a four-by-four grid of squares immune to flexes? Figure 16.2 shows two ways to brace such a grid with only seven diagonals. But one of the braced grids is not rigid. Can readers tell which one?

The answer can be deduced in the following manner. Make up a diagram composed of two sets of dots. The first set represents the four rows of the grid, one dot per row. Likewise, the second set corresponds to the four columns. For each of the seven diagonal bars in the grid, connect the appropriate dots in the diagram. For example, if there is a diagonal bar in the square situated in the third row and the fourth column, then draw a line from the third dot in the first set to the fourth dot in the second set.

Whether the grid is now rigid can be answered by asking the following question: Is the dot diagram connected? In other words, is there a continuous path from any dot in the diagram to any other? If (and only if) so, the grid is rigid. This elegant theorem — first proved by Henry Crapo of the INRIA near Paris and Ethan D. Bolker of the University of Massachusetts at Boston — can help readers quickly determine whether a grid will flex. The diagram for the grid on the left in Figure 16.2 is connected, but the other is not. As an exercise in rigid thinking, I will leave readers with the problem of using the Crapo-Bolker theorem to decide why seven is the minimum number of bars necessary to brace the grid. As far as I know, there is no corresponding theory to advise readers, or my father, about how to brace scaffolds or other cubic grids.

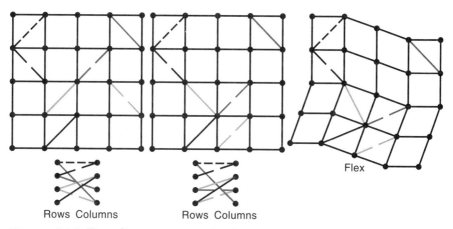

Figure 16.2 Dot diagrams reveal whether a grid is rigid (*left*) or not (*center* and *right*).

Sometimes the search for rigidity requires flexibility in the literal sense. No story better illustrates the point than the history of the famed rigidity conjecture. In the 17th century the French mathematician Augustin-Louis Cauchy wondered whether all convex polyhedral surfaces were rigid. Such surfaces include the triangulated polyhedrons of Alexandrov's theorem and many more. Their facets, or faces, are bounded by plane polygons with any number of sides. Being convex, they have no indentations or hollows of any kind. In 1813 Cauchy proved that a convex, polyhedral surface is rigid if all its faces are triangles. The theorem meant that any convex surface one could construct from triangles, each triangle sharing each of its bars with one other triangle, would be rigid.

Despite the restriction of Cauchy's theorem — that the surface be convex — mathematicians were beginning to wonder whether all surfaces composed of triangles were rigid — even those surfaces that were not convex. Such surfaces may appear to be folded, twisted, or contorted in quite crazy ways. The only requirement was that they be simple in the topological sense. If suddenly converted to rubber and inflated, they must be (more or less) spherical. Additionally, a simple surface required that no part of it touch another part of the same surface. Mathematicians conjectured that if a surface had all these properties, then no matter how deformed it happened to be, a version composed of triangles would suffer no flexes.

For more than a 100 years, no one was able to prove this so-called rigidity conjecture, nor could anyone disprove the conjecture by finding a flexible, nonconvex surface made of triangles. The strongest supporting evidence for the conjecture came in 1974, when Herman R. Gluck of the University of Pennsylvania showed that "almost all" such surfaces were rigid. In other words, examples counter to the conjecture, if they existed, would be rare indeed. Even a contrarian would find this much evidence in favor of a conjecture discouraging.

But Robert Connelly of Cornell University was convinced in some corner of his being that the rigidity conjecture was false. After visualizing surface after surface that looked as though it should flex, Connelly realized one day that he was working against Gluck's theorem. His office was full of models sent to him by amateur mathematicians who claimed flexibility for them. Gluck's theorem said, in effect, "Not likely!" Faced with the same difficulty, Connelly decided to examine mechanisms, namely, frameworks that he knew would flex.

Starting with a very simple flexible framework, he employed his knowledge of topology, spanning parts of the framework with simple tri-

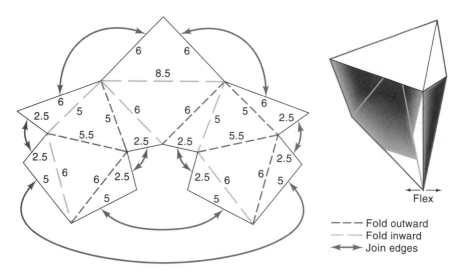

Figure 16.3 How to construct a Connelly-Steffen surface.

angles. Then one day he felt close. Before him was a nonconvex surface that flexed. But it was not quite what topologists call a sphere. Two edges within the surface touched each other, like a deflated basketball in which one side is pressed against the other. The thing was distinctly annoying. So near and yet so far.

It was then that the idea of a crinkle came to him. He suddenly thought of a way to introduce a subdivision of the annoying edges and surrounding triangles that amounted to a fold — enough to take the two lines out of contact. The model he built flexed!

The counterexample to the rigidity conjecture appeared in the litera-ture in 1978. Shortly after, the German mathematician Klaus Steffen found an even simpler surface, based on Connelly's idea, that flexed. Readers who would like to flex their own version of the Connelly-Stef-fen surface will find it laid out in Figure 16.3. To obtain a size that is easy to work with, readers should interpret the edge numbers as centimeter lengths. Arrows that connect the edges in pairs indicate attachments to be completed by armchair rigidity theorists.

When the Connelly-Steffen surface is completed, the two central tri-angles make a fold by which one hand may grasp the surface from above. With the other hand, it will be possible to reach up under the model and then (delicately!) to flex the bottom vertex from side to side, but only by a small amount, roughly 10 degrees.

When this tiny flex is performed, the surface bounds the same volume. These days Connelly ponders whether the constant volume property holds true for all flexible, nonconvex surfaces made of triangles. If he conjectures that they do, he himself may have to be flexible. Some young upstart may find a counterexample.

As something of an upstart myself, I gave my father some trouble over the collapse of the scaffolding. But within a few hours of the accident, the scaffolding was up again. It was identical to the previous structure, except for one extra spruce pole. My father climbed the scaffold confidently. I am sure the tiny wobbles I detected were merely infinitesimal flexes.

Further Reading

Jay Kappraff. *Connections: The Geometric Bridge Between Art and Science.* McGraw-Hill, 1991.

17

AUTOMATED MATH

The whole machinery of our intelligence, our general
ideals and laws . . . are so many symbolic,
algebraic expressions.

GEORGE SANTAYANA, *The Sense of Beauty*

There is an old vaudeville comedy routine that pokes good fun at
the strong-man act familiar from the circus and the state fair. A heavily
muscled man takes the stage with his not so heavily muscled female assistant. The man strains mightily against an enormous weight, and after
tremendous effort he manages to lift it above his head. The spectators
cheer, but the cheers turn to laughter when the assistant casually picks
up the weight in one hand and carries it offstage.

There are two computer programs that leave one with a similar sense
of comic deflation over the mental "muscle" allegedly displayed by a
high score on the traditional I.Q. test. Both programs perform at or near
genius level on two tasks widely used in the tests, the completion of numerical sequences and the perception of visual analogies. Yet both programs are simple to understand, and it is startling to realize just how
dull-witted they are.

Although I have no wish to offend readers who suppose themselves
plentifully endowed with mind stuff, I am twitting the I.Q. test with a serious purpose. The stated intent of the test is to measure intelligence,
and few human qualities evoke such pride in their presence or anxiety
over their absence as intelligence does. Nevertheless, the concept of intelligence presupposed by the traditional I.Q. test is seriously mis-
guided. The reasoning behind this assessment is cogently set forth by
Stephen Jay Gould of Harvard University in his book *The Mismeasure of
Man* (see Further Reading). What it comes to is this: The traditional I.Q.

test rests on the unstated and erroneous assumption that intelligence, like strength, is a single quality of human physiology that can be measured by a graded series of tasks.

Numerical-sequence completion is a good example: What is the next number in the sequence 2, 4, 6, 8, . . . ? In the sequence 2, 4, 8, 14, . . . ? In the sequence 1, 2, 6, 24, . . . ? The percentage of correct responses to a set of such questions measures your "general intelligence," just as a strain gauge measures the weight you can lift and therefore the strength of your arm muscles. Note that if the results of the I.Q. test are to be interpreted as a measure of "general intelligence," there must be some core ability, or some small set of core abilities, that provides an index of what one means by general intelligence. Because the very idea of general intelligence presupposes a strong correlation among the core abilities, the precise kind of graded task adopted by the I.Q. test is relatively unimportant. One task is as good as another.

One of the I.Q. programs presented here is derived from a more elaborate program written by Marcel Feenstra, a student living in Rotterdam. Feenstra's program is called HI Q, and it solves two kinds of numerical problems that often appear on standard I.Q. tests: sequence completion and numerical analogies. Feenstra tested HI Q on a number of sample I.Q. tests that appear in a book by Hans J. Eysenck of the University of London, *Know Your Own I.Q.* (see Further Reading). The I.Q. of HI Q is apparently in the neighborhood of 160. Although the experiment was not exactly a carefully controlled one, it leaves little doubt that the program would score quite well under real test conditions.

The program I have in mind is called SE Q, and it duplicates HI Q's performances on numerical-sequence completion. Readers who write and run SE Q may consider their own numerical intelligence amplified, as it were, by proxy. The main idea of the program is straightforward. When one is given a sequence of numbers and told to find the next number in the sequence, one does not search for the number directly. Instead one searches for the rule that led to the numbers already present. There is a mathematical aside to be made here: For any finite sequence of numbers, there are infinitely many rules that give rise to it. The search thus boils down to finding a simple rule for generating the sequence.

There are just two kinds of rules considered by SE Q: additive and multiplicative. For example, to find the next number in the sequence 2, 4, 8, 14, . . . , one might look for an additive rule, and the best way to find the rule is to construct what I call a difference pyramid (Figure 17.1). At the bottom of the pyramid is the given sequence, and the pyra-

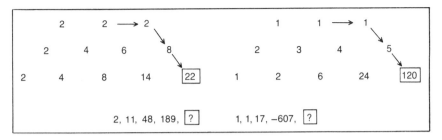

Figure 17.1 Numerical-sequence completion by the pyramid method. Can the reader solve the lower two?

mid is built up from bottom to top by finding the differences between successive numbers in the preceding level or row of numbers. Thus the first number in the second row of the pyramid is obtained from the first two numbers in the first row, namely 2 and 4. Their difference is 2, and so 2 is the first number in the second row. Similarly, the other numbers in the second row are 8 − 4, or 4, and 14 − 8, or 6; the second row is the sequence 2, 4, 6. Continuing the same process to a third row of the pyramid gives a sequence with only two numbers, and they are both 2's.

The equality of all the numbers in some row of the pyramid is the signal, so to speak, to stop building the pyramid upward and to start building it sideways. For example, suppose the third number in the third row is also 2. It is then reasonable to suppose the next number in the second row is obtained from the preceding number, namely 6, by adding 2: the sum is 8. the newly derived number in the second sequence can then be added to the last number given in the first sequence: 14 plus 8 is 22, and 22 is indeed given a perfect score by the test makers. New numbers in each sequence percolate down the pyramid once a constant sequence is derived at the top.

A great many questions on I.Q. tests about numerical sequences yield to this simple procedure. Readers who have more than a nodding acquaintance with algebra will recognize the signature of a polynomial in the exercise. Any polynomial evaluated for consecutive integers yields a sequence that generates a difference pyramid. Given enough values of the polynomial, a row of identical numbers will eventually top off the difference pyramid. The number of rows needed to build the pyramid up to a constant row, minus 1, is the degree of the polynomial. The sequence 2, 4, 8, 14, which gives rise to a constant row of 2's in the third level of the difference pyramid, is generated by successive values of the quadratic, or second-degree, polynomial $x^2 − x + 2$.

Unfortunately one cannot solve all sequence questions by making difference pyramids. For example, the sequence 1, 2, 6, 24, . . . yields a difference pyramid with the numbers 3 and 14 in its top row. The rapid growth of the numbers, however, strongly suggests a geometric series: the consecutive terms of a geometric series are related by multiplication instead of addition. Hence it seems reasonable to construct a set of quotients from the sequence instead of a set of differences (Figure 17.1). By taking quotients of successive pairs in the sequence 1, 2, 6, 24, . . . one obtains the second row in a pyramid, the sequence 2, 3, 4, ... The second sequence hints at an abrupt rule change: the third row in the pyramid must be obtained by taking differences, not quotients. Who can doubt that the intended solution requires a 5 at the end of the second row? The solution itself is thus 120: the product of 24, the last given number in the first row, and 5.

The sequence-solving program SE Q attempts to build pyramids by considering both the consecutive differences and the consecutive quotients of successive pairs of numbers in a given row. Even more, it examines successive pairs of numbers in a sequence for more general additive and multiplicative rules. In the additive rule the first member of each pair may be multiplied by a constant k before the usual addition is done, and in the multiplicative rule the constant k may be added just after the usual multiplication. Here is an easy piece for programming novices (Figure 17.2).

The few simple formulas that give the general rules make up the core of SE Q. Suppose the given sequence has already been assigned to the four variables $a(1)$, $a(2)$, $a(3)$, $a(4)$. To obtain the second row, $b(1)$, $b(2)$, $b(3)$, SE Q tries substituting either a generalized difference, of the form $b(1) \leftarrow a(2) - k \times a(1)$, or a generalized quotient, of the form $b(1) \leftarrow [a(2) - k]/a(1)$. In both examples k stands for any integer in some predetermined range. The program also tries analogous substitutions for $b(2)$ and $b(3)$, each for the same value of k: for $b(2)$ it tries $a(3) - k \times a(2)$ or $[a(3) - k]/a(2)$, and for $b(3)$ it tries $a(4) - k \times a(3)$ or $[a(4) - k]/a(3)$.

The third row, $c(1)$, $c(2)$, is developed even more simply: SE Q tries substituting only simple differences, $c(1) \leftarrow b(2) - b(1)$ and $c(2) \leftarrow b(3) - b(2)$, or simple quotients, $c(1) \leftarrow b(2)/b(1)$ and $c(2) \leftarrow b(3)/b(2)$. Apparently it is rare for sequence-completion questions on I.Q. tests to get more complex than the formulas allow for.

When SE Q develops a pyramid, it tries each generalized substitution for the set of b's with each simple substitution for the set of c's. Conceptually, therefore, SE Q is made up of four major segments. Each segment

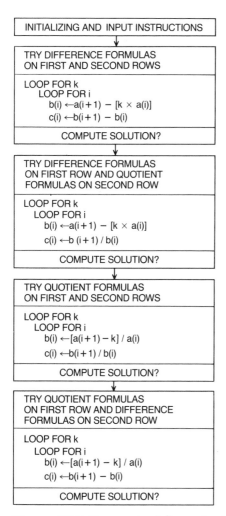

Figure 17.2 Conceptual flow chart for SE Q.

is a loop with one combination of substitution formulas in it. For example, one such segment of the program first applies the three generalized quotient formulas, of the form $b(1) \leftarrow [a(2) - k]/a(1)$, to compute the values of $b(1)$, $b(2)$ and $b(3)$ that make up the second row of the pyramid. The program segment then applies the two simple difference formulas, of the form $c(1) \leftarrow b(2) - b(1)$, to obtain the values of $c(1)$ and $c(2)$ that make up the third row. The complete set of five formulas in this segment is embedded in what might be called a try-everything loop, in which different values of k are tested. Feenstra recommends allowing k to take on all integer values from -5 to 5.

Within the loop, each time new values for $c(1)$ and $c(2)$ are computed they are tested for equality. If they prove to be equal, their common value is stored in a variable called c and the current value of k is saved in a variable called kk. Just after the loop there are instructions that construct the solution to the original sequence (if one has been found) from the values of c and kk. In the example I am describing one obtains $b(4)$, the new member of the second row, by adding c to $b(3)$. The solution, $a(5)$, is then obtained by multiplying $a(4)$ and $b(4)$ and adding kk to the product.

Two instructions at the end of each loop thus suffice to recover a solution from a successful search within the loop. The instructions appropriate for each loop depend on the formulas used in it, and I shall leave it to those who write SE Q to discover the instructions for themselves. Use a bit of algebra to isolate the variable of interest. In each case, if one of the loops in the program finds a solution, there must be an instruction to print it. The program may then skip the remaining loops and stop, or it may execute all the loops in an effort to find more than one solution. By executing all the loops Feenstra has detected several "bad" I.Q. questions that have more than one solution. If none of the four loops finds any solution, it is reasonable to include an additional output statement following the entire lot. The message it prints can vary according to taste; those who like to invest their programs with a little personality can have it print "Help!"

One can try out SE Q on questions from sample I.Q. tests found in several widely available books. In Eysenck's book there are eight complete I.Q. tests, which allegedly enable the reader to discover his or her own I.Q. The tests incorporate several different kinds of questions that appear on standard I.Q. tests, including questions that involve a missing number, a missing letter, a missing word, an odd-man-out, scrambled words and visual analogies (Figure 17.3). A few sub-types are usually found within each major category. For example, in Eysenck's book there are three kinds of questions that ask for a missing number, namely the ordinary numerical-sequence problems I have already described and two other kinds typified by the following examples:

164	(225)	286
224	(——)	476
8	3	21
6	5	25
12	2	—

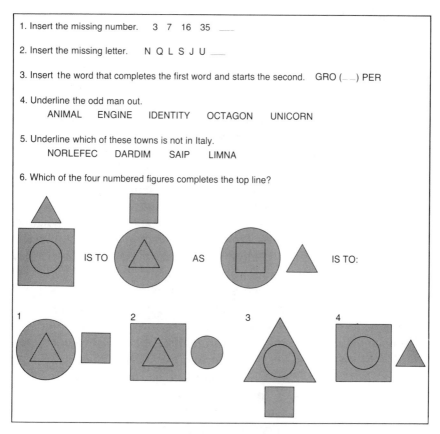

1. Insert the missing number.   3 7 16 35 ___

2. Insert the missing letter.   N Q L S J U ___

3. Insert the word that completes the first word and starts the second.   GRO (___) PER

4. Underline the odd man out.
   ANIMAL   ENGINE   IDENTITY   OCTAGON   UNICORN

5. Underline which of these towns is not in Italy.
   NORLEFEC   DARDIM   SAIP   LIMNA

6. Which of the four numbered figures completes the top line?

IS TO   AS   IS TO:

1   2   3   4

Figure 17.3 I.Q. minitest based on questions from Hans J. Eysenck's *Know Your Own I.Q.*

In each case the would-be genius must supply the missing number in accordance with some perceived rules. Feenstra's HI Q program handles such questions by procedures that draw on the same kinds of formulas as the sequence-completion program does. I encourage readers to try them. Answers to the problems above, as well as others, appear at the end of this chapter.

Although HI Q answers only one major kind of I.Q. test question, the solutions to other kinds of questions can also be mechanized. In fact, a program that solves visual analogies was written more than 25 years ago by Thomas G. Evans as part of a Ph.D. dissertation done at the Massachusetts Institute of Technology. Heavy as it sounds, the essential ideas of Evans' program are easy to understand.

The visual analogies it solves all have the same form: figure A is to figure B as figure C is to one of, say, four figures listed as potential answers. The program selects the analogous figure by first determining a simple set of rules that can transform figure A into figure B (Figure 17.4). It then repeats the procedure with figure C and each of the four potential answers; in each case it generates a set of rules that can transform figure C into the potential answer. The figure obtained from the transformation rules that most closely resemble the rules for transforming figure A into figure B is selected as the solution.

Evans' program repeats essentially one operation five times. Two figures at a time, a source figure and a destination figure, serve as input. For each pair of figures the program then develops a three-part tabular description of how the source figure becomes the destination figure. First the program lists the spatial relations among the parts of the source figure; it then lists the spatial relations among the parts of the destination figure. Both descriptions consider only three spatial relations, *above, left* and *inside*. Finally, the program describes how parts of the source figure change into parts of the destination figure in one of four basic ways: each part can be altered in size, rotated, reflected, or deleted.

Suppose figures A, B and C each have three parts, a circle, a square and a triangle. In figures A and B the program may label the triangles a, the squares b and the circles c, but it makes no attempt to label the parts of figure C in the same way. Instead it arbitrarily assigns the labels x, y, and z to the three parts of figure C. It then develops its three-part tabular description for the pair of figures A and B and four more descriptions, one for each pairing of figure C with a potential solution. The last four tables all employ the labels x, y, and z throughout.

The final operation of Evans' program is to make every possible substitution of a, b, and c for x, y, and z. Since x, y, and z can be permuted in only six ways, there are six substitutions to be tried. One of the substitutions may convert the tabular description of the pair of figures A and B into the corresponding tabular description of figure C paired with one of the potential answers. The figure in this pair is the solution. Even if no perfect matches are found, however, the program can score the relative success of an analogy and so pick the substitution that yields the best match.

Patrick Henry Winston describes the visual-analogies program in his book *Artificial Intelligence* (see Further Reading.) Winston states that the program "works well," and he attributes its success to the use of an effective framework for representing knowledge about the geometric fig-

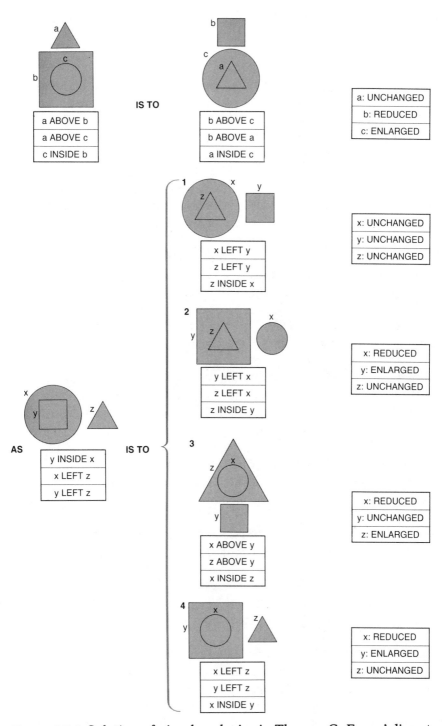

Figure 17.4 Solution of visual analogies in Thomas G. Evans' dissertation.

ures considered by the program. For example, instead of specifying how relations such as *above, left*, and *inside* change from picture to picture, the program might have described how one figure in the first picture gets transformed into another figure in the second. Such a program might be extremely cumbersome, not to say ineffective, because it would have to check a much larger number of potential substitutions than Evans' program does. Indeed, the search for a good representation is a major theme of artificial intelligence: it is often the key that enables a computer to mimic some aspect of human problem solving.

By analogy the representation of objects in the mind is also the subject of much discussion among cognitive scientists. In this context the study of artificial intelligence is often justified as an attempt to exhibit an "existence proof" for the mechanistic description of human capabilities. Thus, goes the argument, if a computer program can be made to simulate some aspect of human behavior, the representation of the behavior adopted by the program at least could serve as the underlying representation adopted by the brain. Nevertheless, it often seems that successful simulations of such behavior give little insight into how people do the same things. For all one knows there may be no relation whatever between the way Feenstra's or Evans' I.Q.-test programs perform and the way people solve the same kinds of problems. Presumably human intelligence deploys more general strategies in attacking particular problems.

This point brings me full circle to the reconsideration of human intelligence: what it is and how it is measured. As I have noted, Stephen Jay Gould has characterized I.Q. as a mismeasure of man. His criticisms carefully document two major fallacies that underlie the concept: the uncritical reification of an abstraction and the ranking of the reified abstraction along a single scale. Language itself accounts in large part for our tendency to make things of what are at best nebulous abstractions. Moreover, once we have persuaded ourselves that we are dealing with a thing, our reflex is to measure it.

In demanding a single numerical measure we succumb to the second fallacy, namely ranking. We want to reduce complex phenomena to a single scale. Such practices have led to excellent physics, but they have also led to some poor social science. I.Q. testing is a case in point; it is to the 20th century what craniometry was to the 19th. In both instances entire racial groups found themselves mismeasured not only because the measure was almost meaningless to begin with but also because there were biases introduced (either consciously or unconsciously) in the process of measuring.

Gould vigorously attacks biological determinism, the idea that human behavior is determined by genes, and he warns against viewing the capacities of our brains as direct products of natural selection. "Our brains are enormously complex computers," he writes. "If I install a much simpler computer to keep accounts in a factory, it can also perform many other, more complex tasks unrelated to its appointed role. These additional capacities are ineluctable consequences of structural design, not direct adaptations. Our vastly more complex organic computers were also built for reasons, but possess an almost terrifying array of additional capacities — including, I suspect, most of what makes us human."

With this last metaphor Gould has put his finger on what I find most unsettling about a relatively simple computer program that can score at the genius level on an I.Q. test. Does the score on the test measure the intelligence of the computer? If it does not, just how does one go about measuring the intelligence of a computer, whether it is made of silicon and plastic or of carbon and tissue? The answer: Probably not by running some I.Q. program through a battery of tests.

Answers to the Minitest and Other Questions

The first problem on the minitest is a good example of the ambiguity typically found in such problems. The problem was to complete the sequence 3, 7, 16, 35,. . . . Each term minus twice the preceding term gives the sequence 1, 2, 3, the second row of a pyramid. By this reasoning the missing term must be twice 35 plus 4, or 74. On the other hand, if a simple difference pyramid is constructed with three rows, the third row gives the sequence 5, 10, and it seems reasonable to complete the sequence with 15. The missing term must then be 69, but the programs described in this chapter would have missed this answer. The other answers to the test: *H* is the missing letter; the missing word is "up"; the odd man out is "identity"; the unscrambled name of the town not in Italy is Madrid, and the correct visual analogy is number 2.

The two numerical sequences are completed by 350 and 22 respectively. The first sequence can be solved by applying a generalized difference rule, with k equal to 3, and then a generalized quotient rule; the missing term is 324. The second sequence ought to defeat all but the most patient puzzle solvers who did not try to write SE Q. It can be solved by two quotient rules; the value of k in the first rule is 5. The missing term is $-65,551$.

Further Reading

Hans J. Eysenck. *Know Your Own I.Q.* Penquin Books, 1982.
Stephen J. Gould. *The Mismeasure of Man.* W. W. Norton, 1983.
Patrick Henry Winston. *Artificial Intelligence*, 2nd ed. Addison-Wesley, 1984.

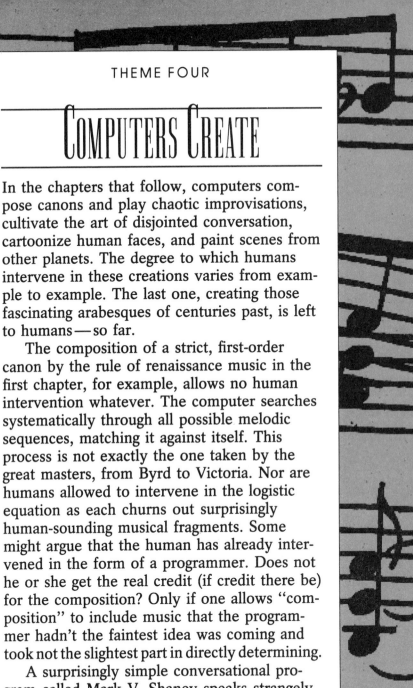

COMPUTERS CREATE

In the chapters that follow, computers compose canons and play chaotic improvisations, cultivate the art of disjointed conversation, cartoonize human faces, and paint scenes from other planets. The degree to which humans intervene in these creations varies from example to example. The last one, creating those fascinating arabesques of centuries past, is left to humans — so far.

The composition of a strict, first-order canon by the rule of renaissance music in the first chapter, for example, allows no human intervention whatever. The computer searches systematically through all possible melodic sequences, matching it against itself. This process is not exactly the one taken by the great masters, from Byrd to Victoria. Nor are humans allowed to intervene in the logistic equation as each churns out surprisingly human-sounding musical fragments. Some might argue that the human has already intervened in the form of a programmer. Does not he or she get the real credit (if credit there be) for the composition? Only if one allows "composition" to include music that the programmer hadn't the faintest idea was coming and took not the slightest part in directly determining.

A surprisingly simple conversational program called Mark V. Shaney speaks strangely to other humans over a computer network. Some think it is a secret AI project that got out of control, others think it is a demented person trying to get attention by saying strange things. But Mark V. Shaney merely echoes the word groups of earlier conversants. It weaves these together into a fabric of speech that reflects our thoughts fragmentarily, like a bad memory of something we said at a party (and now regret). What fascinates people about this program is its marvellous economy of means. It has only a tiny fraction of the length of much more ambitious—and hardly more successful—conversational programs. Perhaps it is a comedian.

The next two programs presented here depend heavily on humans. From a massive file of actual faces, the first program may compile an average face, then use the average face, to create a cartoon of any face in its file. The human, at least, makes the selection. A cartoon in this case is just the face extrapolated in "face space" through point-by-point comparison with the average face, an exaggeration by formula. The second program, really a package of programs, uses geometry and a very powerful graphics computer to render creatures that never were and, one hopes, never will be.

At the end lie the graceful latticeworks from medieval Islamic tombs, monuments, and mosques. How did their artisans discover these brilliant figures? Before anybody programs them, readers have a perfect right to follow the advice of the final chapter to create a special pattern of his or her own. Is this art? This depends on how well it's done.

As for the earlier computer-generated sounds, words, and images, the question is harder to answer. For one thing, no one seems exactly sure what art is or isn't. But critics who commit themselves to gung-ho postmodern cybernetic realism will undoubtedly cheer each new creation from the sidelines. Others, made of sterner stuff, will take an extraordinarily long time to convince.

18

THE COMPUTER COMPOSER

Il est certain que la premierè qualité d'un compositeur,
c'est d'êtve mort.

ARTHUR HONEGGER, *Je suis compositeur*

I t was in 1965 that I first heard the sound of computing. An IBM 7090 at the University of Michigan Computing Center had been fitted with a simple electromagnetic pickup connected to a loudspeaker. As a computer program ran, a specific register in the machine changed its contents many thousands of times per second. The resulting pattern of miniature clicks was heard as an astonishing rush of alien sound that alternated among buzzing, screaming, burping, rumbling, and whining. At times a grinding noise would change from bass to treble. This may have been the sound made by a double loop in the program; perhaps the inner loop executed ever faster, creating a tone of increasing pitch. It all sounded like a humpback whale.

The experience has suggested a variety of programs that explore aspects of melody, harmony, and rhythm. Even though home computers do not normally come equipped with electromagnetic pickups poised over accumulator registers, the majority have small loudspeakers connected to a primitive tone generator. There are instructions in most popular computer languages that call forth a variety of sounds when they are executed. Such a simple facility can be exploited both to make programs audible and to make audible programs. In the former case a sound-generating instruction is added to a program originally intended for computational purposes. I shall discuss this topic briefly later. In the latter case a program is deliberately constructed to produce melodic, harmonic, or rhythmic effects. Two of the programs described here resemble the former kind; a few sound-generating instructions are inserted in otherwise normal-looking code.

Melody, considered merely as a succession of notes, is easily generated by a program. In fact, the program can consist of a single loop. A decision process embedded in the loop decides what note to play next and how long it should be played. The process itself may be arbitrarily complicated. For all I know there are already programs of this type that generate convincing melodies in a given traditional style. If such programs exist, I should be glad to hear of them. In the meantime I shall take the tack of letting available algorithms shape the melody.

The humblest applicants for the job of melody maker are simple arithmetic algorithms. The numerical output of such algorithms is easily converted into notes under an enormous variety of possible encodings. The simplest of the encodings uses the linear congruential assignment, a process that is shorter than its own name:

$$x \leftarrow (a \cdot x + b) \bmod m$$

Here, when one specifies the parameters a, b and m in advance, an initial value of the variable x is converted into a succession of values by the continued iteration of the assignment. The expression "mod m" is an abbreviation for "modulo m," which means that the number computed inside the brackets should be treated like the hours of an m-hour clock. For instance, 10 modulo 8 equals 2. Thus if m is 8 and if a, b, and the initial value of x are all integers, one obtains a sequence of numbers ranging between 0 and 7.

The resulting sequence of numbers is readily converted into a succession of notes by a simple table:

```
0  1  2  3  4  5  6 7
do re mi fa sol la ti do
```

In the program I call SOLFEGGIO (from the practice of sightsinging) the quantities symbolized by the names of the notes are replaced by the frequencies, in cycles per second, of the C-major musical scale beginning at middle C (Figure 18.1):

```
 0    1    2    3    4    5    6    7
262  294  330  349  392  440  494  523
```

Note	C	C#	D	D#	E	F	F#	G	G#	A	A#	B	C
Frequency	261.6	277.2	293.7	311.1	329.6	349.2	370.0	392.0	415.3	440.0	466.2	493.9	523.3

Frequencies of notes above or below this octave are obtained by multiplying or dividing by 1.05946 and rounding off as appropriate. The number is $\sqrt[12]{2}$, the twelfth root of two.

Figure 18.1 Frequencies of the semitone scale from middle C to one octave above middle C.

The complete program can be summarized in the usual algorithmic form:

```
input a, b, x
for i = 1 to 100
x ← (a · x + b) mod 8
note ← notes (x)
play note
```

In my version of SOLFEGGIO the numbers in the figure called *notes* are employed directly by the instruction that generates a tone of the appropriate pitch. Most languages also allow the duration of the tone to be controlled. For the present it will suffice to set the duration to, say, half a second.

A world of maniacal melody now awaits those with an "ear" for arithmetic. Depending on what numbers are selected for the three parameters, one hears either boring staccato monodies, odd, repetitive melodies on a few notes, or strangely wild music full of leaps and sudden runs. In the last category I have been caught short on occasion by not having made a note of the parameters responsible for a haunting little piece forever lost. The algorithm I have suggested produces melodies 100 notes long. Explorers of this new musical terrain may wish to shorten the length in order to investigate more possibilities.

SOLFEGGIO can and should be enhanced. Choose a larger value for the modulus m, large enough to embrace two or more diatonic octaves. There is no modal restriction as such; instead of diatonic scales one can choose 12-tone scales consisting of half-note steps. One can even choose the ultra-modern form of linear-congruential music in which the numbers x produced by the algorithm specify frequencies more directly by the addition of a constant, say 100. If at one point x is 183, then 283 is the frequency of the note the program will play. I wonder what other possibilities readers might invent for themselves. In the meantime here is an interesting question about boredom. For given values of a, b, and m, how many notes will be played before the melody begins to repeat itself?

Harmony is now within the vocal competence of many home computers. Those equipped with two or more speakers will be able to play the entire repertoire generated by a program I call CANON. Indeed, a few enthusiasts will undoubtedly carry the project much further. Some readers may already have acquired a MIDI. The acronym stands for Musical Instrument Digital Interface, an electronic black box that converts signals generated by one's computer into commands for electronic instruments such as musical keyboards and individual synthesizer channels. (Readers interested in learning more about MIDI may write the International MIDI Association, 12439 Magnolia Boulevard, Suite 104, North Hollywood, Calif. 91607.)

CANON generates two-part harmony involving two almost identical melodic lines. Rounds such as "Row, Row, Row Your Boat" and "Frère Jacques" exemplify the type if not the species. CANON generates a canon in the academic tradition known as first-species imitation, a first stage in the serious study of counterpoint.

Such a harmony has two melodic lines that satisfy four criteria. First, all notes have the same duration. Second, one line begins after the other. Third, both lines are identical except that one line is transposed upward by some standard musical interval (unison, perfect fourth, perfect fifth, or octave). Fourth, the two lines together must satisfy, note for note, certain rules of first-species imitation. All the rules are found in standard texts. Such rules generally include the allowed note-for-note harmonic intervals (Figure 18.2) and establish the shape of participating melodic lines. In the interest of simplicity the latter has been omitted.

An example of a harmony in first-species imitation is shown in Figure 18.3. The example was written by a human being, not by a machine. A glance makes it plain that after a certain point the composer tires of the strenuous demands imposed by all four criteria. Rule three is usually the first to go; it is enough if the second line imitates the first in spirit only.

A computer program, on the other hand, is undaunted by the constraints. CANON will grind on tirelessly until an entire piece is generated. The usual output of the program is tedious, however. To avoid this problem I have generated a great many short canons and have catalogued the more interesting ones. Some of these may then be strung together to make longer pieces (Figure 18.4). The experiment was done a

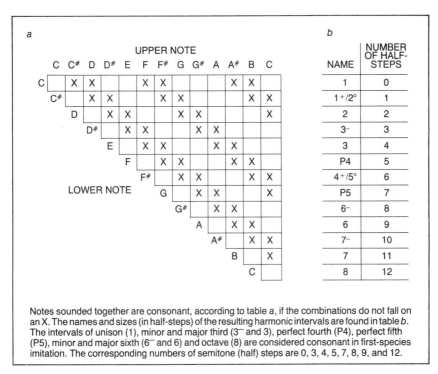

Notes sounded together are consonant, according to table *a*, if the combinations do not fall on an X. The names and sizes (in half-steps) of the resulting harmonic intervals are found in table *b*. The intervals of unison (1), minor and major third (3⁻ and 3), perfect fourth (P4), perfect fifth (P5), minor and major sixth (6⁻ and 6) and octave (8) are considered consonant in first-species imitation. The corresponding numbers of semitone (half) steps are 0, 3, 4, 5, 7, 8, 9, and 12.

Figure 18.2 Table of consonant harmonic intervals.

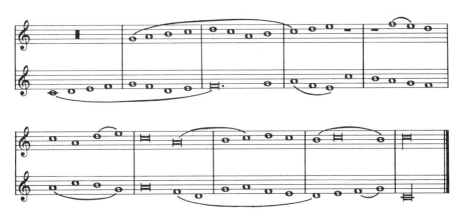

Figure 18.3 Example of first-species imitation.

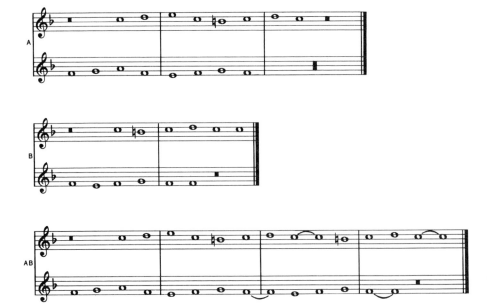

Figure 18.4 Two computer-generated canons are spliced to make a larger one.

decade ago with the assistance of Gregory Utas, one of my students at the University of Western Ontario.

CANON counts its way into a piece. Suppose, for example, it has been told to generate a miniature canon six notes long. For reasons that will soon be obvious, the tonal range spanned by each musical line is small, say six chromatic steps up and six steps down from the tonic, or beginning note. The set of 13 possible notes can be thought of as digits in a base-13 number system. The digit 0 represents the tone six steps below the tonic and the "digit" 13 represents the tone six steps above. CANON proceeds quite simply by counting its way through all six-digit base-13 numbers. Each one, after all, encodes a melody of a kind.

Every time CANON generates a new melodic line it makes a copy, transposes it upward by a fifth, and translates it forward by a specified number of notes, say two. It then compares the pairs of notes brought into temporal juxtaposition by the operation. If none of the resulting pairs violates the rules of harmony, the line is accepted as canonic and is either printed out directly to the waiting composer or saved in a file for later printing.

In particular, CANON requires that the composer specify three parameters before running the program: *int*, the interval of imitation, *del*, the delay in starting time for the second melodic line, and *num*, the number of notes in each line. The notes of the line being generated are stored in an array called melody, or *mel* for short. Here is an algorithmic outline of CANON:

```
input int, del, num
mel(1) ← 7
for i = 2 to num
    mel(i) ← 1
found ← false
while found false
    increment mel
    for i = 1 to num − del
        compare mel(i) and
            mel(j + del) + int
    if harmonious then found ← true
output mel
option to continue
```

The algorithm starts by assigning to *mel*(1), the first note of the canon, the value 7. This is the tonic note, and it will not change. The remaining entries in *mel* all start at the value 0. A while loop tests a Boolean, or logic, variable called *found*, which is initially set false. *Found* is made true if a valid canonic melodic line is discovered by the instructions in the body of the loop. First, the array *mel* is incremented. This can be done by scanning the array from right to left. In the process of scanning, the counting procedure looks for an array entry that is less than 13. On finding such an entry, it adds 1 to it and changes all the entries to the right (if there are any) to 0. This is precisely what happens in ordinary counting, where 9 replaces 13. For example, $3572 + 1 = 3573$, $3579 + 1 = 3580$ and $3599 + 1 = 3600$.

The next job of the loop is to compare each note *mel*(j) with the note *mel*($j + del$) + *int*. In other words, the program adds *int* to the note that is *del* notes after *mel*(j) and looks up the difference of the two note values in the table of rules for first-species imitation. If the difference is considered harmonious in all cases from 1 to *num* − *del*, the Boolean variable *found* is made true. (The notes beyond *num* − *del* are played alone with no accompanying harmony. Thus there are no note differences to look up in the table.) Once such a melodic line is found and printed out, the program asks the composer, "Do you want to continue?" If the answer is yes, the program branches back to the *found* ← false instruction and the count picks up where it left off.

One can, of course, play the melodic lines discovered by CANON through the tiny loudspeaker of one's home computer. Readers of a musical bent, however, will develop the knack of humming the line or of transcribing it, along with its canonic companion, onto sheet music. The canon can then be tested at another keyboard in all its harmonic glory.

Rhythm is a more sophisticated musical form that some readers may realize; traditional Western music has never been very elaborate rhythmically. Popular musical culture, on the other hand, has embraced an extraordinary variety of rhythmical forms (Figure 18.4). Most of them originate either directly or indirectly from traditional African or Asian music. This includes most rock music, jazz, Caribbean, and Latin-American music. Westerners are also increasingly aware of the complex contribution of the tablas (a pair of drums played by the fingers) to Indian musical forms such as the raga.

The program I call BEAT enables one to spedify simple rhythms as sequences of 0's and 1's (Figure 18.5). These are translated into sounds by the simple expedient of running through the sequence repeatedly. Each time through, the presence of a 1 triggers a brief tone pulse. A 0 triggers nothing.

Actually BEAT is simple enough to describe without further ado. Structurally it is rather similar to SOLFEGGIO (the program that plays linear-congruential music). A single array called *pulse* holds the rhythm as specified by the programmer at the start of the run:

```
input pulse, num, dur
for i = 1 to 25
  for j = 1 to num
  k ← 1
  while k ≥ dur
    k ← k + 1
  if pulse(j) = 1
    then sound
```

The variables called *num* and *dur* refer respectively to the size of the input array and the duration between sounds. The outer loop specifies that the basic rhythmic interval determined by *pulse* will be played 25

Figure 18.5 Four sample rhythms for BEAT.

times. This number can easily be altered by readers who stumble onto rhythms they would like to hear for a longer period of time. The next inner loop controls the array index; the algorithm will consider each entry in turn in order to decide whether or not to play a tone. How long to wait between sonic events? That much is determined by a special waiting loop that simply counts up to the specified duration, *dur*. Then, if *pulse(j)* is 1, the program BEAT will play a tone, a buzz, or whatever may be available. If *dur* is small, the rhythm will be fast. If *dur* is large, the rhythm will be slow.

Like its predecessors, BEAT can also be enhanced. Something like a percussion ensemble is possible if different tones (preferably low ones representing various kinds of drums, bells, or cymbals) are employed. Although the sounds may be far from realistic, the rhythms will be the real McCoy. One can complicate the array called *pulse* by using integers such as 0, 1, 2 and 3 to represent silence, a high drum playing alone, a low drum playing alone, and both drums playing together. In each case the entry of *pulse* being examined in the inner loop must be decoded by a set of if statements that control the playing of no sound, one sound, or both sounds. In the last case two notes are sounded consecutively as a substitute for simultaneity. If it is found that playing two consecutive sounds throws the timing off, then the waiting loop must be moved inside the if statements so that there is one copy for each of the four possibilities. In the case of no sound and two sounds, the limit *dur* must be replaced by new limits, one longer and one shorter than *dur*. In both cases the difference would be the time value assigned to an individual note.

A more sophisticated version of BEAT will certainly be able to play some of the interesting rhythms displayed in Figure 18.4. The various scores shown there have been interpreted as sequences of discrete events strung along a common time base. They are easily translated into the contents of *pulse* under encodings arranged by the aspiring composer.

In addition to the preceding forays into melody, harmony, and rhythm, I continue to be fascinated by the notion of endowing every computer program with two rules. In one role the program computes what it computes. In the other role the program is fitted with a tone or two next to its inner loops, outer loops, and conditional (if) statements. The program has a song to sing for each problem it is given. Those who listen regularly to their favorite program (be it recreational or commercial) will develop an ear for its performance. I have no doubt that some bugs in new versions of a program may be detected by ear. The programmers will thank me for putting this bug in their ear.

19

CHAOS IN A MAJOR

Extraordinary how potent cheap music is.

NOEL COWARD, *Private Lives*

Few readers have heard of Victor Chaosky. His music has an other-worldly quality that is hard to describe. But critics have yet to call it un-musical. His *April One Suite*, though played by a single instrument that sounds at times suspiciously like the tone generator on a home computer, leaves no doubt of the composer's brilliant, chaotic talent.

Some people have attempted to imitate the music of Chaosky, all with amazing success. One of these is Arthur Davidson, a low tempera-ture physicist at IBM's Yorktown Research facility in Yorktown Heights, NY. He uses the famed logistic equation, the simplest chaotic system known, to produce the notes from his personal computer, an IBM PC running turbo Pascal. He notes that more than one visitor to his office has remarked (in almost the same words on each occasion), "Say! Isn't that Philip Glass?"

They may have heard of the composer Glass, but not, evidently, of Victor Chaosky. From time to time, Davidson runs the program he calls CHAOS IN A MAJOR (or CHAOS-A for short), listening intently. This is the sound of chaos reduced to a manageable scale. Interesting musical patterns seem to repeat themselves with slight variations when, sud-denly and unaccountably, they change gears as if Chaosky had aban-doned his theme in mid-passage, inspired by a new musical idea. But the patterns are not merely musical. Can Davidson hear in them a hint of or-ganization to be exploited or learned from? Among his missions at IBM Research, he studies non-linear dynamics, the behavior of physical or mathematical systems that do not have a linear response to their state variables, but a non-linear (e.g. quadratic) one.

As a child, Davidson had studied the violin and still likes to "fool around" on the piano. "Anyone who has heard me will tell you that I am not a musician," he says. A few years back, Davidson was heavily involved with the logistic equation, staring at the famed map by day and, as usual, playing around with musical scales in the evening. "Eventually, I got the idea to put the two things together." The rest is history of a sort that some future student of simultaneous invention may want to explore: At the same time, others were trying exactly the same idea.

There are a few versions of the logistic equation, all equivalent. The one favored by Davidson has the fewest symbols in it:

$$x \leftarrow x(a - x)$$

I have put the equation in the form of an algorithmic assignment statement so that readers may see more clearly what the equation "does." The current value of the variable x is subtracted from the parameter a and the result is then multiplied by x. In the final step, the value just computed replaces the previous value for x and the whole process begins anew. To make a short story miniscule, when you put this statement inside a loop and translate the resulting sequence of values into musical notes, a wonderful new composition by Chaosky emerges.

The logistic equation does not represent a real-world physical system as such, although it vaguely echoes the behavior of a predator-prey dynamic; the more there is of x, the less there is of $a - x$. The logistic equation represents only the simplest version of an infinite number of non-linear dynamical equations some of which describe the behavior of real-world systems and some of which do not. Since the phenomena to be probed are in a sense common to all such systems and since the phenomena are primarily mathematical in any event, it is not particularly important that they be "real." Chaos is chaos.

In the logistic system, the presence or absence of chaos depends on the choice of value for the parameter a. Ranging from 1 to 4, this parameter alone will determine a remarkable number of different behaviors. At $a = 1$, for example, no matter what starting value of x less than a is chosen, the sequence determined by the logistic equation will converge rapidly to a single value (Figure 19.1). This represents an equilibrium value for the system, like a vibrating string coming to rest in a single position. There is a way to visualize the process precisely. In Figure 19.2 readers will see a set of nested parabolas. Each parabola represents the quadratic

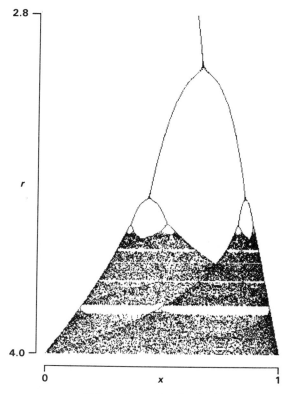

Figure 19.1 What does the logistic map sound like?

equation that results when a different value of *a* is frozen. Take out a pencil and ruler and try the following experiment on the smallest parabola, the one labelled 2.9.

This parabola represents the dynamics of the logistic system when *a* = 2.9. Starting with any value you like on the *x*-axis between 0 and 2.9, draw a line straight up to intersect the curve, then from the point of intersection rule another line across to meet the diagonal. This defines another point, and from that point draw a third line vertically to intersect the parabola again. Continuing to draw this sequence of horizontal and vertical lines that connect the diagonal and the parabola, you will see a pattern emerge. A square spiral of line segments will converge on a specific point of the parabola. All of the vertical lines in the sequence repre-

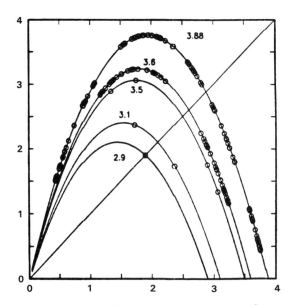

Figure 19.2 Each parameter value produces new musical possibilities.

sent successive values in the logistic formula. The horizontal lines represent iterations of the equation. In the parabola labelled 3.1 two points are marked. These comprise a two-point attractor representing the equilibrium behavior of the system when $a = 3.1$. Successive parabolas yield a geometric interpretation of what is happening in the logistic system at certain values of the a-parameter. The largest parabola is a sample of chaotic behavior. Only 100 points are shown but if the iteration had continued, the parabola would soon be black with them! Chaos.

This situation corresponds to a slice across the bifurcation diagram in Figure 19.1 at the level $a = 3.88$. On the way to chaos, readers who simply write a program that produces and plots successive values of the formula as points on a horizontal line will notice the well-known period-doubling phenomenon.

If your program is written to accept different values for a from the keyboard, then to run the equation for, say, 100 iterations, it will produce values that converge on a one-point attractor for any a up to approximately 3. After that a two-point attractor shows up. For example, at 3.1 successive numbers bounce back and forth between two limiting values, converging to them. At $a = 3.5$, there is a four-point attractor. At still higher values there is an eight-point attractor, a 16-point attractor, and so on. The period doubling builds up at such a frantic pace that long before *a* gets very much bigger than 3.6, the system begins to behave very strangely. Suddenly, the attractor consists not of some power of two but of an infinite number of points. The attractor is no longer simple but "strange." Here is where music enters the picture—literally!

If you play with the program I have just described, you will notice, as Davidson did, that when *a* is increased above 3.57, the chaotic points spread out to cover more and more of the parabola. Davidson's description of what he saw is colorful enough to repeat.

"Now in playing around with these things on a PC, I noticed that iterating the map in the chaotic regime would not exactly repeat a value, but it would frequently almost repeat a value. In fact it would almost repeat whole sequences of values." (see Figure 19.3.) "Aha! This is where I heard the bell ring. It was exactly how I had come to regard music! To maintain your interest, music must represent some sort of pattern that you recognize. . . .

As Davidson goes on to say, variations in the pattern will sustain the interest even longer. This made an entirely new program necessary. He

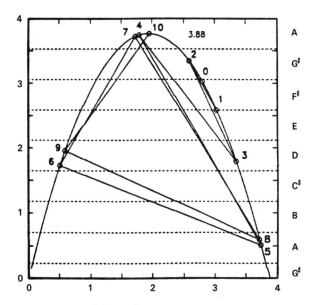

Figure 19.3 Map of a tone sequence.

divided the range of x-values up into subranges, one for each note in the diatonic (major) scale from A to A. Then he set to work.

A bare bones chaos composition program can be written on the basis of a seven-line algorithm. Inside a loop which may be one of several types, including even a simple for-loop, iterate the logistic equation once, translate the value produced by the equation into a frequency, then play the tone that corresponds to the frequency. Figure 19.4 shows the essential steps based on a repeat loop that can only be terminated when the user presses a key.

Within the loop, when the next value of x is calculated, it is converted into an integer between 0 and 12 called *step*, then into a frequency called *tone*.

The notation in which this last calculation is expressed leans slightly in the direction of turbo Pascal. Essentially, a base frequency of 220 Herz (middle-A on the musical scale) is multiplied by 2 to the power of *step*/12. The function called exp denotes taking a power of the transcendental number e, then correcting with a factor of ln(2), the natural log of 2. So much amounts to a power of 2 and what follows is just the power taken, namely, *step*/12. If step = 0, the base note , A, remains the same. If step = 1, the result is 220 multiplied by 2 to the power of 1/12. This is one-twelfth of the way up the semitone scale from A to the A one octave higher. Thus, when step = 12, the frequency of 220 is multiplied by 2 to yield a frequency of 440, an octave above 220.

---

input x and a

repeat

    x ← x*(a − x)

    step ← int(12*x/a)

    tone ← int(220*exp(ln(2)*step/12))

    play tone

until key pressed

Figure 19.4 Chaotic music algorithm.

The twelve-tone semitone scale will sound just a bit too "modern" for some readers. To get a more pleasing diatonic scale, the basic calculations must be changed. First, the value of x will have to be transformed into an integer between 0 and 8 (0 and 7 will serve about as well). The resulting number, step, will then be converted to a tone by adding an integer that causes the appropriate semitones to be skipped. Under this arrangement, the needed tones are: 0 (A), 2 (B), 4 (C#), 5 (D), 7 (E), 9 (F#), 11 (G#), 12 (A). The problem of writing the one or two lines of code that will convert *step* into *tone* can, I think, safely be left to most readers.

How do you get sound out of your system? Davidson uses the turbo Pascal command called "Sound." Specifically, Sound (220) or more generally, Sound (freq) will produce a tone of middle A in the first case and a tone of whatever frequency happens to be specified by the variable *freq* in the second case. In order to hold the tone for a time, Davidson inserts a delay loop ("delay(n)" in turbo Pascal, where n is in milliseconds). The sound must, after this delay, be turned off. The next step in CHAOS A will therefore be the turbo Pascal command "Nosound." Anyone programming in BASIC can use a somewhat simpler command: SOUND freq, dur. By this I mean that SOUND is a function that has two arguments. The first argument, whatever you call it, is either a number or a variable that specifies the frequency in Herz of the desired note. The second argument specifies the duration in "clock ticks," each BASIC clock tick lasting approximately 1/18 of a second.

There are a dozen useful features that can be added to the basic CHAOS A program to make it a genuine tool for the intellect, not to mention a flexible music maker. Here is what Davidson's version of the program does:

1. makes a musical graph of the notes being played
2. interactively allows new values of *a* to be entered
3. gives the user the option of supressing the music
4. gives the user the option of transposing the music up or down

Davidson is the first to admit that the program can be developed well beyond this point. In fact, there is no need to stick to the logistic equation. There is a wonderful book by Francis Moon (see Further Reading) that lays out a number of other simple equations, including one based on the circle. I await the results of reader programs with bated breath, as does Davidson.

Fuguette végétarienne

Steffen Schindler & Ralf D. Tscheuschner

Figure 19.5

Who else has tried a chaos music program? Ralf D. Tscheuschner at the Institute for Theoretical Physics in the University of Hamburg, for one. Tscheuschner, a physicist, has collaborated with Steffan Schindler, a computer science graduate student at Hamburg, to produce an interactive music composition system based on the logistic map. Of all the chaotic music I have heard, these compositions seem the most musical. After all, they incorporate the human touch, getting the best of both worlds from chaos and the human musical mind. I have included a sample composition of theirs (and the program's) entitled *Fuguette Végétarienne* (Figure 19.5). Not Chaosky's work but, one would have to say, inspired by it.

With such profound musical developments, who can doubt that the music of Chaosky (in one form or another) will soon reverberate from thousands of homes and offices!

Further Reading

Francis C. Moon. *Chaotic Vibrations*. John Wiley & Sons, 1987.

20

MARK V. SHANEY

When I meet someone on a professional basis, I want
them to shave their arms.

MARK V. SHANEY, net.singles conversation

In Boston on a chilly November day in 1991 a press of media milled
about the auditorium at the Computer Museum, a converted warehouse
in the Boston harbor district. The museum, which houses the world's
largest exhibition of computer history and hands-on displays of computer technology, was hosting the first annual Loebner Prize Competition. In another room of the museum ten judges communicated via type-
written messages with entities that were either computers or humans.
Their job: Decide which. It was the first public trial of artificial intelligence based on the famed Turing test.

The Loebner prize, established by New York businessman Hugh G.
Loebner, was to be awarded to the program that fooled more of the
judges than any of its competitors. In this restricted form of the Turing
test, the topics of discussion were strictly limited. The judges, ordinary
people off the street, were policed by referees who were experts in computing and artificial intelligence.

In the grand auditorium, ten screens displayed the conversations as
they progressed. Each screen displayed the text flowing through a particular terminal. And whether the terminal was connected at the other end
to a distant human or computer, the domain of discourse appeared as a
label on the screen: fishing, women's clothing, martini making, personal
relationships, small talk, the plays of Shakespeare, whimsical conversation, and so on. Every eighteen minutes, each judge got up, moved to a
new terminal and began a new conversation. He or she carried a score

pad on which each entity would ultimately be ranked from most human to most computerlike. Behind the scenes museum officials wrung their hands and muttered. There had been an hour delay setting up some of the lines to long distance participants. What if no program fooled any of the judges?

The audience moved from screen to screen, laughing here and groaning there. Some people had no doubt that the screen for terminal five (labeled whimsical conversation) belonged to a program:

JUDGE: Hello! You seem to be feeling quite witty today.

TERM: Hello, judge, what is your mood today? happy? sad? ready for some fun? Hello — how's the weather up there today? Let's talk about psychology!

JUDGE: It has been a long day! Now I think I'm ready for some fun. The weather isn't very pleasant today. Do you have any jokes that could lift the clouds?

TERM: Everybody talks about the weather but nobody seems to do much about it. Why do you need to tell me you think you're ready for some fun? Groannnnnn. . . .

JUDGE: Well you did ask me!

TERM: Now you have really outdone yourself in asking stupid things! Woof . . . woof . . . woof. . . . Why do you think I did ask you?

Other members of the audience who watched this screen weren't so sure. Perhaps it was a human going "woof, woof." Some humans, after all, are better than others at whimsy.

If the entity behind screen five was a computer, who could doubt that the entity behind screen four (the plays of Shakespeare) was a human?

JUDGE: Tell me what your favorite Shakespeare play is.

TERM: *The Tempest*, how about you?

JUDGE: *Julius Caesar.*

TERM: Ah, of course, that play would better be called *Brutus*, but the title of *Julius Caesar* was and is more saleable.

JUDGE: Why do you think it would better be called *Brutus*?

TERM: Because it's about Brutus! Caesar dies pretty quickly, and except for his death scene he hardly has any scenes. Maybe Shakespeare played Caesar, he always wrote himself a nice little role to play.

Here it seemed obvious that the entity behind screen four was meeting the questions and comments of the judge head on, so to speak. As this and other conversations with judges revealed, the entity was quite knowledgeable about Shakespeare in a way that expert systems, even equipped with all the same facts, could hardly express in fluent English. By the same token, however, audience members who were less conversant with computers and AI were more willing to believe that its extensive knowledge betokened something of the superhuman, something of the computer, in other words.

Museum officials needn't have gnawed their nails about the outcome. Five of the judges ranked the whimsical conversant on the human side of a line that was supposed to separate the humans from the computers. All was revealed at the end of the Loebner Prize competition as cameras whirred and flashbulbs crackled. Headlines could now read:

COMPUTER FOOLS HUMANS

The winner was a program called PC Therapist, the creation of Joseph Weintraub of Woodside, N.Y. Specializing in whimsical conversation, the program is meant to beguile the hours of lonely or depressed people with a kind of rollicking if somewhat evasive companionship. The cash award on this inaugural event was a mere $1500. In a later competition, when the full Turing test is to be implemented, the award will climb to $100,000. But only if a program takes at least one (expert) judge the distance in a more or less unlimited topic area. But never mind the small award. As one reporter whispered to another at the edge of the crowd, "He'll clean up on this!"

PC Therapist resembles the famous program Racter. Racter, short for "raconteur," is a Fortran program that uses immense files to create chains of association that, over the short term at least, give the impression of topic orientation. But like Racter and like Eliza, the famed psychotherapeutic program before it, PC Therapist frequently gets the grammar wrong when it attempts to mirror statements made by the hapless user.

"Oh, you say you think I are evading the question!"

In view of these shortcomings, it seemed a little unfair to some of the AI experts who refereed the contest that there should have been a category called whimsical conversation in the first place. It gave an unfair advantage to any program entered in it. Whimsy, after all, is a very broad and forgiving category. Who is to say that grammatical errors shouldn't be a part of whimsy? Evasion and frequent topic changes also take a more or less natural place here and an inexperienced judge is all the more prone to fall prey to a program that asks about the weather and goes "woof woof."

But the potential of whimsical conversation is something that future entries in the Loebner Prize Competition might want to take advantage of. Enter a potential candidate.

Some years ago, the bulletin board service called Net.Singles was invaded by an obstreperous program called Mark V. Shaney, the brainchild of Don P. Mitchell and Bruce Ellis, then with the AT&T Bell Laboratories in Murray Hill, New Jersey. Ellis and coworker Rob Pike had noticed the banalities of typical Net.Singles postings and thought it might be fun if Mark V. Shaney were unleashed as a participant.

First, however, Mark had to be fed substantial volumes of typical postings. This was quite easy to do since they were already in machine readable form. Mark scanned the text of these conversations, building a rather large table in the process. For every pair of words that occurred in the conversations on dating, make-up, mixed marriages, and related topics, the table developed a series of entries, once for every word that followed the given pair.

For example, the pair "find a" might be followed, here and there in this large volume of text, by words such as "date," "person," "dollar," and so on. Some follower words would occur more frequently than others and for each of these the table would contain a probability based on frequency. Thus if the word pair "find a" occurred 7 times in the text and it was followed 3 times by "date," then the table entry opposite the ordered triple (find, a, date) would be $3/7 = 0.429$. And so with all other pairs of words and their followers in the text.

Simple in principle, Mark V. Shaney consists of two parts, a table builder and a text generator. After scanning an input text and constructing the table of follower probabilities, Mark V. Shaney is ready to "talk." It begins with a single pair of words. The generating algorithm is simple.

repeat
    $r \leftarrow$ random
    determine pair follower
    output follower
    first $\leftarrow$ second
    second $\leftarrow$ word
until someone complains

When a random number r is selected, it determines a follower by the process of adding together the probabilities stored for each of the words that follow the given pair until those probabilities first equal or exceed r. In this way, each follower word will be selected, in the long run, with a frequency that reflects its frequency in the original text. And in this way, the text so generated bears an eerie resemblance to the original:

"When I meet someone on a professional basis, I want them to shave their arms. While at a conference a few weeks back, I spent an interesting evening with a grain of salt. I wouldn't dare take them seriously! This brings me back to the brash people who dare others to do so or not. I love a good flame argument, probably more than anyone . . .

"I am going to introduce a new topic: does anyone have any suggestions? Anybody else have any comments experience on or about mixed race couples, married or otherwise, discrimination forwards or reverse, and eye shadow? This is probably the origin of make-up, though it is worth reading, let alone judge another person for reading it or not? Ye gods!''

Mark V. Shaney can continue virtually forever in this vein, spewing out an endless Markov chain (hence the name) of probabilistically determined word followers.

Network opinion did not take long to crystallize. Mark V. Shaney was either a severely disruptive individual, not to mention a psychopath, or else it was someone's pet AI project that had got out of hand. As one complainer put it: "Will someone please pull the plug on Mark V. Shaney?" Given Mark's relative success on Net.Singles, might there be some hope for a near relative in next year's Loebner Prize Competition? It all depends on what I mean by a "near relative."

The table of letter followers created by the Mark V. Shaney program is three-dimensional because every pair of words in a received next has one or more followers that are also words. But what is true of pairs of words is also true of triples. Every triple of consecutive words that occur in the text is followed by a *fourth* word. This suggests that one might construct a four-dimensional table and generate, in consequence, text that is even closer to the language of the received text.

There is no reason, of course, why a second-order Mark V. Shaney could not be constructed to operate on triples of words rather than single ones. Let us call her Shirley Shaney. I expect that Shirley will sound somehow more sensible than her disruptive brother. Readers with a modicum of programming skill have enough advice to build a Shirely Shaney. Warning: Once Shirley is written and debugged, she will require rather large volumes of text to get started. An entertaining form of input would involve conversations between Shirley and her maker. Cycles of table building would alternate with sentence generating while Shirley slowly "learned" her creator's conversational pattern. At such a pass her creator could then watch for the announcement of the next Loebner Prize Competition.

FACE SPACE

The face is unmistakable. There are the low, floppy ears, the prominent cheekbones, the high pompadour. Ronald Reagan's face is familiar around the world, but somehow it is even easier to spot his likeness in a caricature than it is in a photograph (Figure 21.1). Surely the art of caricature calls for deep insight into human nature. If this be the stuff of computation, surely the computer is a trivial adjunct — little more than a sketch pad — that merely stores the highly subtle renderings of the caricaturist in a visual form.

Or is it? The caricatures on these pages were all generated by a program devised by Susan E. Brennan, a staff scientist at the Hewlett-Packard Laboratories in Palo Alto, Calif. To run the program a mouse, a light pen, or some other analogue of a pencil might be convenient, but they are certainly not essential. The results depend hardly at all on a steady hand or a practiced eye. Instead, once a photographic likeness of the face is entered into the computer, the program takes over and draws the caricature. How is it done? A short answer is deceptively simple: the program compares the photograph of the target face with an average face stored in the memory of the computer. The features that differ most from the average face are scaled up in size.

Brennan's program followed naturally from her own considerable abilities as a caricaturist and her interest in the cognitive processes underlying face recognition. Such processes have long baffled psychologists and cognitive scientists, and caricatures seem to play a special role

205

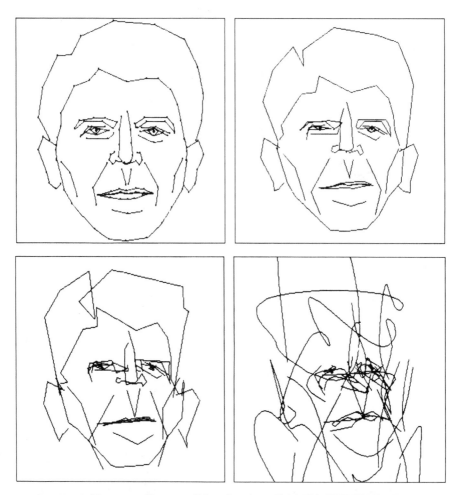

Figure 21.1 From realism to "facelessness" in FACEBENDER, a program based on the work of Susan E. Brennan, with stops for caricatures of Ronald Reagan in between.

in the process because when they are recognized, they are recognized almost instantly. Could it be that instead of remembering a friend's face, we remember a caricature of it? To address these issues Brennan invented her simple technique for generating caricatures, and she described it in her master's thesis at the Massachusetts Institute of Technology. She continues that interest in her spare time; in her working hours she now experiments with new forms of communication between human and computer that rely in part on natural language understanding.

Conceptually Brennan's technique is closely related to a trick that computer animators call in-betweening. Imagine two drawings of familiar objects, such as an apple and a banana, both done by connecting dots with lines (Figure 21.2). Each dot on the apple is then paired with a dot on the banana. If the paired dots are also connected by lines, the midpoints of the lines depict a brand-new fruit that splits the difference between the apple and the banana—a banapple, of course.

The same lines that connect the apple and the banana can also give rise to an extreme form of the banana—from the point of view, so to speak, of the apple. Extend each line beyond the banana by half its original length and then place dots at the end of the lines. When the dots are connected, the banana emerges in caricature. Similarly, by projecting the connecting lines beyond the apple, one can obtain a caricature of an apple—from the point of view of the banana. Faces can be treated in much the same way. Each pair of faces defines two mutual caricatures. The best caricatures, however, arise from comparison with a norm, or average face.

The norms in Brennan's program are made up from sets of several dozen real faces in a data base of several hundred. Points are chosen that outline the features of each face, and the points are labeled with respect to a set of matrix-based coordinate axes. The origin is at the upper left of the image plane, and the coordinates increase from left to right and downward. The scale is adjusted so that the left pupil is at the point (135, 145) and the right pupil is at the point (190, 145). The coordinates of corresponding points on each face are averaged to give the norm for that point. For example, the combined coordinates of the outer corner of the left eyebrow give the average coordinate for the outer corner of the eyebrow of the average face. Three norms are constructed in this way: there is an average male face, an average female face, and an average, overall plain-vanilla face. It is no surprise that the plain-vanilla face looks somewhat androgynous; it establishes the norm for most caricatures (Figure 21.3).

To draw a caricature based on the norm, the program must be supplied with a digitized version of a real face. In practice the face begins as a photograph, and the program prompts the user in turn for each of the 186 key points on the photograph. For instance, when the program calls for the six points that make up the left eyebrow, the user can respond by

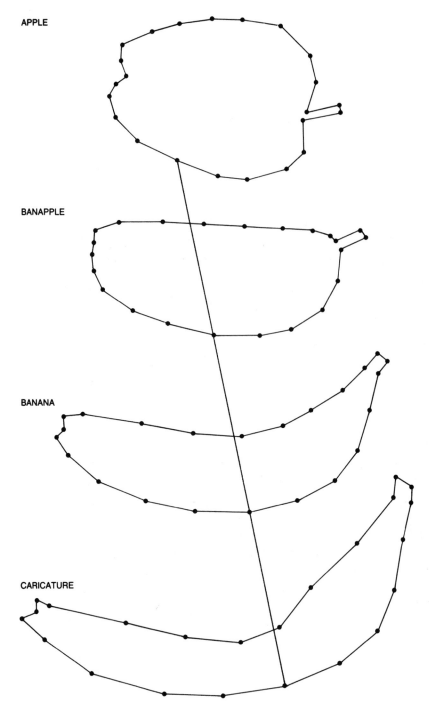

APPLE

BANAPPLE

BANANA

CARICATURE

Figure 21.2 How to turn an apple into a banana, and beyond.

Figure 21.3 The androgynous average face.

moving a mouse to successive points on the left eyebrow of the photographic image on the screen.

It is useful to think of Brennan's program as a fast shuttle for exploring what she calls face space. The entered coordinates for the points defining a photograph can be strung together in a predetermined order. The result is a list of numbers that can be treated as coordinates of a single point in a high-dimensional space. For example, both the average faces and the photographic face are represented by 186 points, each of which has two coordinates. The resulting list of 372 numbers for each face is a point in a 372-dimensional space. In principle every face can be assigned to a point in face space, and any two faces in face space can be connected by a straight line.

There is no need to be mystified over the concept of a higher-dimensional space. Face space is merely a handy abstraction for describing differences and similarities among faces. The familiar concepts of the straight line and the distance between two points have straightforward analogues in any higher-dimensional space. All the points along a straight line in face space represent proportional changes in each coordinate value. The distance between two points in face space is a measure of their similarity: similar faces are close neighbors in face space, and dissimilar faces are literally farther apart.

In face space one can imagine the norm as being near the center of a cloud of points representing realistic images of real faces. A line joins each real face to the norm. The points along the line correspond to a succession of intermediate faces that look increasingly like the real face. Beyond that face are the caricatures, but there is a natural limit to recognizable exaggeration: the caricatures eventually lose their human qualities and degenerate into a chaotic state Brennan calls facelessness.

The idea that every face is a point in face space suggests another fascinating transformation. Since any two faces in face space can be joined by a straight line, one can ask the program to generate a transitional sequence from one face to another. Brennan finds such sequences particularly intriguing when the two endpoint faces are male and female: the program effortlessly transforms Elizabeth Taylor into, say, the late John F. Kennedy (Figure 21.4).

The reader can duplicate some of Brennan's feats of caricature by writing a smaller version of her program; I call it FACEBENDER. It requires the user to supply at least two faces: a norm and the target face to be caricatured. I have referred above to the norm, whose coordinates have been generously provided by Brennan (Figure 21.5). The user must then convert the target face into the same form. In the absence of sophisticated digitizing equipment the reader can, with relatively little pain, convert a photograph of a loved one (possibly oneself) into a list of coordinates. Brennan warns, however, that the face in the photograph must have a bland, neutral expression; even a slight smile will grow to a monstrous grimace. The face must also be fully frontal; if the head is turned, FACEBENDER will turn it even more.

To determine the scale for the axes, assume the coordinates of the left and right pupils are the same as the norms: the left should be at (135, 145) and the right at (190, 145). (Remember that horizontal coordinates increase from left to right and vertical coordinates increase downward.) Once the distance scale is established the user must find the rest of the coordinates by careful measurement. In Brennan's digitizing scheme the points on the face are organized into 39 facial features; each feature is a

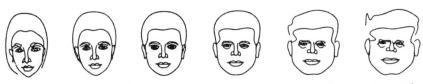

Figure 21.4 Elizabeth Taylor (as Cleopatra) meets former President Kennedy in face space.

succession of connected points. The order of the points depends on the orientation of the feature: for features that are mainly horizontal the points are listed from left to right, and for features that are mainly vertical they are listed from top to bottom.

Brennan admits that identifying the key points on a face is governed mostly by trial and error, but the former president's face can be used as a guide. For this reason it is important that the same person carry out the conversion from photograph to list for each face entered into a data base.

FACEBENDER stores the two digitized faces in arrays called *face* and *norm*. A third array called *disp* is needed to crate a display. All three arrays have 186 rows and two columns: one face point per row and one coordinate per column. Points are arranged in the serial order given in the list for *norm*. The advantage of this ordering is that all lines in the final picture can then be drawn between successive points in the array; of course, lines are not drawn between successive array points when one feature is complete and another is about to be drawn.

The first feature the program draws is the pupil of the left eye; the second feature is the right pupil. Each pupil can be rendered as either a dot or a small circle; somehow the circles look friendlier. For the remaining features, however, lines are drawn to join consecutive points in the array. A special array called *features* is needed to skip the line between the last point in one facial feature and the first point in the next. The array gives the number of points in each feature, and a double loop supervises the skips (Figure 21.6).

Because the first two features have already been drawn, the display routine begins with the third feature, namely the left iris. The first point in the left iris is the third point of the array *disp*, which is indexed by the variable i; hence the value of i is initially set equal to 3. The array *features* is indexed by another variable, j, and it ranges from 1 to 37 because there are 37 features left to draw. Within the j loop another variable called *count* keeps track of the number of lines drawn for each feature; it increases by 1 with each passage through the j loop. The index i is also increased with each passage through the loop; it identifies the point in the array *disp* that is currently participating in the frantic exercise of connect-the-dots.

Inside the j loop is a second loop called a while loop; it compares the number of points joined so far in feature j with the total number of points in that feature. The program leaves the while loop when the two numbers are equal; the feature is complete. If there are still points to connect

Feature	Count							
LEFT PUPIL	1 POINT	(135,145)						
RIGHT PUPIL	1 POINT	(190,145)						
LEFT IRIS	5 POINTS	(134,141)	(128,144)	(133,149)	(140,144)	(135,141)		
RIGHT IRIS	5 POINTS	(190,141)	(184,144)	(189,149)	(196,144)	(190,141)		
BOTTOM OF LEFT EYELID	3 POINTS	(119,147)	(133,140)	(147,146)				
BOTTOM OF RIGHT EYELID	3 POINTS	(177,147)	(190,141)	(203,147)				
BOTTOM OF LEFT EYE	3 POINTS	(121,147)	(133,150)	(147,146)				
BOTTOM OF RIGHT EYE	3 POINTS	(177,147)	(191,150)	(201,148)				
TOP OF LEFT EYE	3 POINTS	(118,143)	(132,137)	(148,142)				
TOP OF RIGHT EYE	3 POINTS	(176,143)	(191,137)	(204,143)				
LEFT EYE LINE	3 POINTS	(127,154)	(135,153)	(144,150)				
RIGHT EYE LINE	3 POINTS	(178,151)	(187,154)	(196,154)				
LEFT SIDE OF NOSE	6 POINTS	(156,140)	(156,153)	(156,165)	(154,172)	(156,179)	(161,182)	
RIGHT SIDE OF NOSE	6 POINTS	(166,140)	(166,153)	(166,166)	(168,172)	(167,179)	(161,182)	
LEFT NOSTRIL	6 POINTS	(150,169)	(147,173)	(146,178)	(148,182)	(153,179)	(161,182)	
RIGHT NOSTRIL	6 POINTS	(173,169)	(176,172)	(177,178)	(174,182)	(170,179)	(163,182)	
TOP OF LEFT EYEBROW	6 POINTS	(112,137)	(113,132)	(125,127)	(139,128)	(150,131)	(152,136)	
TOP OF RIGHT EYEBROW	6 POINTS	(171,136)	(173,132)	(186,129)	(199,128)	(208,132)	(211,137)	
BOTTOM OF LEFT EYEBROW	4 POINTS	(112,138)	(124,132)	(138,134)	(152,136)			
BOTTOM OF RIGHT EYEBROW	4 POINTS	(171,136)	(187,134)	(200,132)	(210,137)			
TOP OF UPPER LIP	7 POINTS	(137,203)	(149,199)	(156,196)	(162,199)	(168,197)	(177,199)	(187,202)
BOTTOM OF UPPER LIP	7 POINTS	(138,203)	(148,203)	(156,202)	(163,203)	(170,202)	(178,203)	(186,202)

TOP OF LOWER LIP	7 POINTS	(138,203) (149,203) (156,202) (163,203) (170,202) (177,202) (186,203)
BOTTOM OF LOWER LIP	7 POINTS	(141,204) (148,207) (155,210) (163,211) (171,210) (179,207) (185,203)
LEFT SIDE OF FACE	3 POINTS	(103,141) (101,160) (104,181)
RIGHT SIDE OF FACE	3 POINTS	(219,140) (222,159) (218,179)
LEFT EAR	7 POINTS	(99,150) (92,144) (88,149) (90,160) (94,174) (99,187) (104,184)
RIGHT EAR	7 POINTS	(224,149) (231,144) (234,151) (232,160) (230,173) (224,185) (219,184)
JAW	11 POINTS	(104,181) (108,199) (115,214) (129,228) (147,240) (162,243) (180,239) (196,228) (207,215) (215,199) (219,178)
HAIRLINE	13 POINTS	(101,144) (107,129) (114,114) (120,104) (131,95) (146,92) (160,93) (174,95) (188,96) (201,103) (210,114) (217,126) (222,143)
TOP OF HEAD	13 POINTS	(93,204) (78,173) (76,142) (82,101) (99,70) (129,46) (158,44) (188,45) (217,64) (236,94) (245,134) (250,168) (233,200)
LEFT CHEEK LINE	3 POINTS	(145,175) (139,182) (135,190)
RIGHT CHEEK LINE	3 POINTS	(178,176) (185,183) (190,191)
LEFT CHEEKBONE	3 POINTS	(105,178) (109,184) (112,190)
RIGHT CHEEKBONE	3 POINTS	(218,178) (214,183) (211,189)
LEFT UPPER LIP LINE	2 POINTS	(159,186) (159,193)
RIGHT UPPER LIP LINE	2 POINTS	(165,186) (165,193)
CHIN CLEFT	2 POINTS	(162,232) (162,238)
CHIN LINE	3 POINTS	(153,218) (162,216) (173,219)

Figure 21.5 The coordinates for the points of an average face.

213

```
DISPLAY ROUTINE                    EXAGGERATION ROUTINE
i ← 2                              for i ← 1 to 186
for j ← 1 to 37                        bend(i,1) ← face(i,1) +
    i ← j + 1                          f*[face(i,1) − norm (i,1)]
    count ← 1                          bend(i,2) ← face(i,2) +
    while count < features (j)         f*[face(i,2) − norm (i,2)]
        draw line from disp(i)
            to disp(i + 1)
        count ← count + 1
        i ← j + 1
```

Figure 21.6 The heart of FACEBENDER.

in the feature, the program draws a line from point i in the array *disp* to point $i + 1$. My notation is merely shorthand. A real display command would call for a line from the point whose coordinates are *disp(i,1)* and *disp(i,2)* to the point with coordinates *disp(i+1,1)* and *disp(i+1,2)*.

The heart of FACEBENDER is its exaggeration routine. Its structure is even simpler than the display routine I have just outlined (Figure 21.6). For each of the 186 facial points in the arrays *face* and *norm*, the loop calculates a new array called *bend*. The new array encodes the caricature-to-be. Each coordinate of the array *bend* is calculated by adding the corresponding coordinate of the array *face* to a quantity that exaggerates the differences between *norm* and *face*. The exaggeration factor f is typed in by the user; f then multiplies the difference between the horizontal coordinates of *face* and *norm*, and it also multiplies the difference between the vertical coordinates.

The only things left to do are to organize the program and, optionally, to tune up the drawing routine. A simple, nonprocedural approach to organization is to place both the display routine and the exaggeration routine inside an interactive loop that asks the user: "Want to try another?" The program must also prompt the user for the exaggeration factor. Arrange the prompt so that a number of different exaggeration factors can be tried without having to reenter the array *face*; their effect on the caricature is then easy to compare.

The drawings can be somewhat enhanced if the dots are connected with so-called spline curves instead of with straight lines. Splines avoid zigs and zags and connect the dots smoothly; Brennan's program usually draws spline curves to form the smooth contours of facial features. Nevertheless, I was aware that splines might prove sticky to explain in a book that is devoted largely to easy programs. I asked Brennan for an alternate method. Could straight lines be used instead? Much to her surprise and mine, caricatures drawn with straight lines proved almost as good as the ones drawn with splines. Indeed, all her images appearing here were drawn using straight lines. With only a small loss in aesthetic value the programmer can avoid a most troublesome technique. One can immediately set about digitizing a favorite photograph.

Brennan's caricature generator has been applied in several studies of facial recognition. Faces from her program have been transmitted over telephone lines as part of an experiment in teleconferencing at the Massachusetts Institute of Technology Media Laboratory. In 1985 she did an experiment with Gillian Rhodes of the University of Otago in New Zealand, who was then a graduate student working with Roger N. Shepard of Stanford University. First she generated caricatures of faculty members and students in the psychology department at Stanford. The caricatures were then tested for recognizability against standard line drawings.

Brennan has summarized the findings: "The caricature generator was particularly useful for this study because it enabled us to generate stimuli that varied in a continuous and controlled way; previous perceptual studies have had to compare caricatures with photos or other kinds of not-so-similar images, and have therefore not been free of representational effects. Caricatures were not found to be particularly *better* as recognizable representations (the 'best' representations were only modestly exaggerated), but when the highly exaggerated caricatures were recognized, they were recognized significantly *faster*— about twice as fast, in fact, as the realistic line drawings of the same people."

Brennan suggests a number of other experiments with the caricature generator. For example, it would be fascinating to recover the "norm" assumed by human caricaturists. Handed a caricature of a given subject by a given artist, she would try reversing the exaggeration to determine the normal face, presumably lodged somewhere in the artist's unconscious mind, from which the exaggeration was derived. Would the reconstructed norm be much the same from one subject to the next? Would different artists assume different norms?

Further Reading

A. K. Dewdney. *The Magic Machine: A Handbook of Computer Sorcery.* W. H. Freeman, 1990.

VOLTAGE SCULPTURES

Sometimes I consider myself a fisherman. Computer
programs and ideas are the hooks, rods and reels.
Computer pictures are the trophies and delicious meals.

CLIFFORD A. PICKOVER, *Computers Pattern Chaos and
Beauty*, St. Martin's Press, New York, 1990.

On the first day of the earth year 2991, the *Armstrong* interstellar spacecraft touched down on the fourth planet orbiting the star Tau Ceti. The *Armstrong's* crew detected movement from the northeast and focused the ship's camera on a distant rocky cliff. There on a ledge was a nest made of rock crystals and an egg that resembled a fried pastry, a French cruller to be exact. The egg began to dissolve, and from it emerged a snakelike creature composed of two intertwined rings. The mission biologist quickly dubbed it a "gorgonoid." As the probe moved closer to get a better look at the gorgonoid, the creature stiffened in fright and bounced off the cliff into an acetylene river.

To be sure, the world of the gorgonoid is science fiction, but its image resides in a computer at the IBM Thomas J. Watson Research Center. Clifford A. Pickover, a graphics wizard at IBM, created the alien I call the gorgonoid to demonstrate powerful, new tools for computer graphics. He has developed the techniques as part of his mission to help other scientists visualize the intricate shapes produced by physical phenomena or derived from theories. Pickover, whose microscopic biomorphs appeared in my book, *The Magic Machine*, describes his creations as "graphics from an unseen world" (Figure 22.1 and color insert).

Although the gorgonoid egg looks like an alien life-form, it is actually a model based on physical principles discovered in terrestrial laboratories. If one could peel away the "shell" of the gorgonoid egg, one would

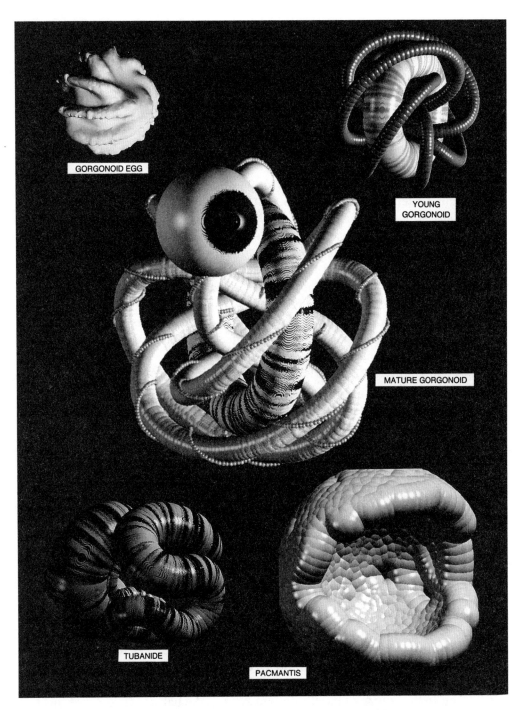

Figure 22.1 Computer creatures from an unseen world.

find a frame composed of two "wires." One is bent into a circle; the other winds around the circle in a spiral that rejoins itself. If the wires were charged with a certain voltage, they would generate an electric force that would be stronger at points close to the wire frame than at points farther away. Pickover's computer program finds all the points representing a given strength of the force and then plots them to form the shell of the gorgonoid egg. Pickover calls this imaging technique volt-age sculpture.

Pickover engages in the art of voltage sculpture to depict a variety of atomic structures from single molecules to the complex spiral of DNA. Because the voltage sculpture displays the electric forces surrounding the molecules, investigators may be able to deduce how some molecules produced by living cells can fit certain receptor sites in other cells.

The young gorgonoid is not a voltage sculpture but what might be called a worm necklace. Like the egg, the gorgonoid is based on two wire loops, one winding around the other. To make the body of the gorgon-oid, Pickover adorns the wires with spherical beads: large ones for the circular wire, small ones for the spiral one. The beads are spaced evenly along the wires, and consecutive beads overlap.

The mature gorgonoid is a worm necklace made of three wires: the first wraps around the second, which in turn curls around the third. The mature gorgonoid also has an eye made from three nearly concentric spheres that intersect to form an iris from one sphere and a pupil from another.

A mature gorgonoid can spot a predator a mile away through an am-monia haze — an important survival strategy when it is being stalked by a pacmantis. This cup-shaped creature spends half its time basking in the rays of Tau Ceti. But when the pacmantis gets hungry, it rolls on the ground, opening and closing its mouth like the computer sprite known as Pac-man.

The anatomy of the pacmantis is no more complicated than the mor-phology of the gorgonoid. To bring the pacmantis to life, Pickover creates a computer pendulum. He simulates a ball that is tied to one end of a rigid wire; the other end is connected to a pivot that allows the wire and ball to swing freely in all directions.

Initially, the pendulum is pushed sideways with a certain velocity and swings down under the influence of gravity. After it swings back and forth, it arrives at a point that is a certain distance away from its starting point. In the course of its subsequent swings, the ball covers most of the available space within the sphere of possible positions.

As the pendulum swings, Pickover's computer periodically takes snapshots of the ball. When many images of the ball are displayed simultaneously, they form a shell. By rotating the shell 90 degrees, one sees the exoskeleton of a pacmantis in its proper orientation.

Although the pacmantis will occasionally munch on a gorgonoid, it prefers to dine on the tubanides that live in ammonia oceans. These succulent shellfish resemble certain ammonoids that flourished on the earth during the Mesozoic era. The tubanide has an attractively striped shell, which begins as a straightforward open spiral but subsequently curves back on itself—like the product of a demented tuba maker. As a result of its twisted shell, the tubanide tumbles as it swims, making it easy prey for the pacmantis.

Tubanides were spawned from Pickover's collaboration with Australian conchologist Chris Illert. Pickover and Illert studied a bizarre ammonoid called *Nipponites mirabilis*. Most ammonoids, like the modern *Nautilus*, have regular, logarithmically spiraling shells that allow the animal to move smoothly through the water. During the early stages of growth, the shell of *N. mirabilis* grows much like that of other ammonoids, but later it twists and turns in all directions. Illert hoped to investigate such unusual growth patterns by searching for a mathematical description of the irregular spiral.

He came up with a formula that has a simple interpretation. The orientation of the opening of the shell determines the direction of the shell's growth. In ordinary spiral growth, the orientation of the opening would remain fixed in relation to the adjacent rings of the shell. But the growth of *N. mirabilis* can be nicely simulated if the shell opening is rotated according to an exponential rule: as the shell grows, the opening rotates more and more. This hypothesis produces a proper ammonoidal appearance for young *N. mirabilis* and yields a twisting, irregular-looking spiral for the older animal.

Pickover and Illert demonstrated that the tubanide is a good model for the adult *N. mirabilis*. To render tubanides in living 3-D, Pickover used the worm-necklace technique. He colored the tubanide by alternating between crimson and white spheres.

The concepts behind worm necklaces and voltage sculptures are as simple as advertised, but I am tempted to add the performer's warning: "Do not try this at home!" After all, Pickover has access to computers specifically designed for graphics. His computer system can automatically shade and hide surfaces; it can show light from several sources reflecting off a surface; and it can produce, in an instant, a view of any three-dimensional object from any angle. The skin of Pickover's creatures is therefore only a few keystrokes away.

Although such facilities are not available in home computers, Pickover would not discourage amateur programmers from creating some exquisite alien graphics called spherical Lissajous figures (Figure 22.2). In 1857 the French mathematician Antoine Lissajous first described these sinusoidal figures that today parade on the screens of oscilloscopes. A single Lissajous curve is traced out on the screen as a bright dot moves up and down and side to side any number of times and eventually returns to its starting point.

Spherical Lissajous figures have the same properties as their two-dimensional relatives, except that they lie on the surface of a sphere. To represent this three-dimensional curve in three dimensions, one needs

Figure 22.2 A spherical Lissajous figure.

three separate equations, each involving a single variable, t, which one can think of as time.

$$x = R\sin(At)\cos(Bt)$$
$$y = R\sin(At)\sin(Bt)$$
$$z = R\cos(At)$$

R, A, and B are constants. For each value of t, the three formulas collectively specify a single point in three-dimensional space. As the value of t is incremented (as time passes), the formula produces a succession of points that generate the spherical Lissajous curve.

By setting values for R, A, and B, the rates at which the curves oscillate, one may generate fascinating figures. The curve will close back on itself unless the ratio of A to B is an irrational number, not a likely event in a computer.

Readers can devise a simple computer program to view a spherical Lissajous curve on a two-dimensional screen. The program should first ask for the values of R, A, and B. The program should then enter a loop where the value of t is increased from, say, 1 to 1,000. For each value of t, the program should calculate x and y according to the formulas. The x coordinate, for example, will multiply R by the sine of A times t, then by the cosine of B times t. Finally, the program should plot the point (x,y).

Some caveats accompany this algorithm. First, the numbers x and y may have to be specially modified so that the point being plotted will appear on the screen. If necessary, add a suitable constant. Second, the values of t may have to change more gradually to produce a solid-looking curve rather than a string of widely spaced points.

Pickover is delighted at the potential of his tools and similar techniques to help not only scientists but also artists. As examples of artists who have already exploited such possibilities, he cites William Latham of the IBM U.K. Scientific Center, John Lewis of the New York Institute of Technology and Donna J. Cox of the National Center for Supercomputing Applications at the University of Illinois at Urbana-Champaign. As electronic devices shrink and get faster still, even computers like Pickover's sophisticated system will find their way into smaller and more affordable boxes. The implications for science and art will be equally great as more and more graphics emerge from unseen worlds.

Further Reading

Clifford A. Pickover. *Computers, Pattern, Chaos, and Beauty*. St. Martin's Press, 1990.

23

LATTICEWORKS BY HAND

Although computers are creeping tone by tone and pixel by pixel into the arts, vast areas of endeavor still remain open to human beings. The designs I call latticeworks are not exhibited on computer screens but rather on ordinary sheets of paper. The latticeworks are not produced in a few seconds by a computer program; they emerge slowly from a ruler and compass guided by the human hand.

The designs begin when imagination meets a grid of circles. Anyone can play and possibly produce an amazing interlocking network of lines that confuses and delights the mind. The designs are similar to those found on ancient tombs, mosques and palaces from Samarkand to Seville. Rectilinear ornaments from the Islamic world of medieval times hint at infinity within a finite space. Did the artisans use the methods I shall describe? Experts are uncertain what method was employed, but the mathematical reverberations of the patterns echo from geometry to topology.

There are many ways to view a latticework, but perhaps a good starting place is to look for symmetry. The finished version of the specimen in Figure 23.1, for example, has a high degree of symmetry: one can rotate it by 120 degrees about certain points and end up with an identical pattern. One can also reflect it across certain lines and get an almost identical pattern. The chief elements of the pattern are gold bands that weave like small highways of thought through a potentially infinite landscape. Throughout the design circles are spaced according to the underlying symmetry of the pattern. The bands travel from one circle to another, converging in 12's and then abruptly bending away. The angle of reflection equals the angle of incidence. The bands themselves have shapes, in this case either hexagonal or zigzag. Everywhere one looks, overpasses alternate with underpasses. By what means was this arranged?

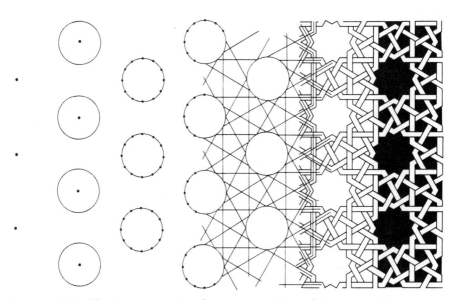

Figure 23.1 Various stages in the construction of latticework.

Latticeworks belong to a wide class of infinite patterns that have at least two independent symmetries of translation: if one translates, or slides, the pattern over a copy of itself in either of the two directions, eventually the pattern and its copy will line up with each other. No matter how cleverly one lays down an infinite pattern, as long as it has two independent translations it will inevitably belong to one of the 17 possible crystallographic groups first classified by the Russian scientist Evgraf S. Fedorov. Considering the enormous wealth of latticeworks inherited from the past, it is not surprising that examples of all 17 groups can be found, whether peeping shyly through a palace window grille or proclaiming the sultan's grandeur in the audience hall.

Translations are just one of four possible symmetry operations that can be done on a plane imprinted with a pattern. A reflection flips the plane like some vast door about a line that lies within the plane itself. This is essentially the looking-glass operation, in which letters get reversed and faces look slightly different. The third symmetry operation is the rotation, and in it the plane is rotated through a specific angle about a single point. The fourth and final symmetry is called a glide reflection. It consists of a translation followed by a reflection about a line that is parallel to the translation.

Symmetry operations (of whatever type) can be combined simply by performing them in some sequence. An algebraic structure called a group emerges from all of this. In a group the product of any two operations is an operation, and every operation has an inverse operation that in effect undoes it. In addition a group has a so-called identity element (the do-nothing operation). A group must also satisfy the associative law: when three successive operations are carried out, it does not matter whether the third operation follows the first two or whether the last two follow the first one. Put this way the law sounds mildly idiotic, but only because the associative law happens to be transparently true in the case of symmetry operations on the plane. The symmetry group of the latticework in Figure 23.1 is called $p6$ in the international crystallographic language. It is characterized by having rotations of 60 degrees about one set of centers and rotations of 120 degrees about another set. Readers will readily find the centers in the figure.

I produced the design a few years ago by the method I shall outline here. Later I discovered the same latticework in a book about Islamic art of the medieval period. My deflation at not being first was more than compensated for by the discovery itself; the method seemed confirmed. Since then it has been my lot to "rediscover" other designs.

The method requires the would-be artisan to set up a grid of points. The grid is limited to one of four types: triangular, square, rectangular or hexagonal. Such grids are easy to lay out by ruler or compass: draw a base line, then use the compass to mark off evenly spaced points. Square and rectangular grids employ a right-angle construction to add new points above and below the base line. Triangular and hexagonal grids require equilateral triangles.

The design under discussion began life as a triangular grid. A circle was then drawn at each of the grid points. Here intuition made its first entrance, because the size of the circle happens to be critical. In a moment I shall explain the role intuition may play in selecting the size.

Once the circles are all drawn, the amateur artisan selects points evenly spaced around the circle. These points will anchor the lineal elements of the design. The position and number of points must reflect the symmetry of the grid itself. In other words, the points should preserve symmetry with respect to reflections and rotations. Any of the intended symmetries should carry points on one circle onto points on another circle or on the same circle. In the example under construction the number of points on each circle must be a multiple of 3. I chose 12 to give body to the lattice. Since the underlying pattern was to have reflectional symmetry, only two positions for the points on the circles were possible. I chose the position in which six of the points were closest to the surrounding circles. As a general rule, whenever there is a choice, the best decisions are those that harmonize with a symmetry already present.

In the next stage of construction one joins the points on each circle to points on other circles. Here intuition makes a second entrance. The possibilities appear to be so numerous that only intuition would seem to serve. In fact, the combinatorial possibilities are greatly limited once more by conditions of symmetry: if I join a certain point on circle A to another on circle B, the symmetries of the pattern carry that connection onto other points on circle A. Before one has drawn more than two lines it may be necessary to erase the experiment and try another connection.

A kind of feedback loop binds this design phase with the earlier choice of circle size. Once a seemingly satisfactory and consistent scheme of interconnection has emerged, the results may look unauthentic, not to mention ugly. The lines do not harmonize with the symmetry of the pattern. In such a case it is usually obvious whether shrinking or expanding the circles will produce connections that parallel the major symmetries of the pattern. Here intuition may provide the leap of insight, a kind of artistic "Aha!" experience. In the mind's eye one suddenly sees the lines generated by the new circles.

At this point in apprenticeship a certain excitement causes the compass and ruler to quiver slightly. An amazement that is perhaps half artistic and half mathematical grips the holder of these instruments. Should one take credit for an intuition that was merely acceding to geometry?

In any event, it is now time to pave the highways of thought by giving them some width. No sophisticated system of roads should suffer traffic lights, and so how can the angular freeways be interlaced? In true weaving, after all, overs and unders alternate. Can the artisan be forced into some kind of logical cul-de-sac where a road faces two consecutive underpasses? Topology saves the day.

The following experiment in scribbling shows how. Draw a large rectangle on a sheet of paper. Then scribble inside the rectangle, abiding by only two rules:

1. If a line begins or ends, it must do so on the boundary of the rectangle.
2. No more than two lines (or parts of the same) may cross at any point.

One can, for example, scribble something like the abstract-expressionist composition shown in Figure 23.2. Lines can be curved or bent, repeatedly crossing over one another.

To convert the scribble into the cleverest knot imaginable, it is now only necessary to follow the "over-under" rule: starting anywhere one likes, simply follow one of the lines, repeating "Over, under, over . . . " Of course, one must make an overpass for the line being followed when "Over" is said. By the same token, "Under" calls for an underpass. Eventually one either returns to where one started or the boundary of the rectangle is reached. En route the line may have crossed itself. Amazingly, whenever one arrives at a previously processed crossing, it already has the required structure. In other words, one never finds that an overpass is called for at a crossing that has already been designated an underpass. Eventually all bridges have been built and the scribble takes on an appearance that is almost intelligent.

The over-under rule works because in a sense it must. The simplest demonstration at a public level invokes a pleasant thought excursion. The scribble divides the rectangle into many small regions, or pieces. It turns out that the regions in the rectangle can each be given one of two colors, so that no two regions sharing a common boundary are assigned the same color. (A convincing elementary proof of this property would take at most a few paragraphs, but I hasten to the punch line.) Suppose the regions are painted in this manner with, say, red and blue paint. Driving along one of the roads toward a crossing, we would notice one of

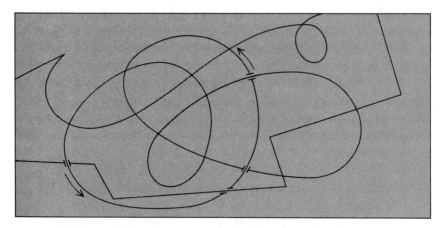

Figure 23.2 The "over-under" rule in progress.

two things: either the region on our right would be red and the one on our left would be blue or vice versa.

The recipe for crossings lurks in this simple observation. Traveling along a given road, the mental construction crew will know whether to build an overpass or underpass when they arrive at a crossing. If the region to the right is red, build an overpass; if it is blue, build an underpass. The result is exactly the same as (or possibly the "negative image" of) the result if the crew had followed the over-under rule stated above.

With a pencil and a ruler the designing reader can easily thicken each line of the latticework by drawing a parallel line on each side of it. At bends there is some fiddling with the meetings of these lines, but the project proceeds more or less mechanically. The thickening procedure may ignore the crossings until they are complete. Equipped with an eraser, the artisan now attacks the crossings, invoking the over-under rule as he or she goes. To create an overpass, one must erase the two segments of road edge that cross the road one travels. As soon as this is done the overpass springs into existence. The road that was erased seems to pass under the road one is on. Underpasses are created by the opposite procedure. It is interesting that the interlacing procedure destroys all reflectional symmetries of the pattern; the reflected pattern may look the same but underpasses and overpasses have been swapped.

The final stages in the creation of a design involve inking and coloring. A good pen will follow the ruler and produce an even line with occasional interruptions at bends and crossings. A design of moderate complexity may take an hour or more to ink, but what is an hour in the timeless world of the artisan? There is time to think of other things during this phase. It is perhaps a loose form of meditation.

When the design has been inked and all the pencil marks have been erased, it can be colored directly. Because coloring does not always turn out as well as one might like, it may be preferable to copy the inked original and color the copy. In this way the original can produce many offspring, each more beautiful than the one before. I suggest using tempera paint. It goes on evenly, produces minimal wrinkling of paper and is available in virtually all colors, including gold and silver. Moreover, water-based paints such as tempera seem to be repelled by xerographic inks. This is fortunate because unless one has a very steady hand, overpainting of ink lines seems inevitable. One wants all colored areas to be finely edged with black in order to enhance contrast.

The colors one selects are of course a matter of personal choice. Authentic latticeworks often employ dark and muted primaries for the regions between the bands. Such treatment results in a retreating background that points up the latticework itself all the more prominently. I have included another design that uses such a color scheme (Figure 23.3).

The second design was produced by methods similar to the first. Advanced latticeworks have not only what might be called primary circles of inflection but also secondary ones. Each five-pointed star in the second design arises from such a secondary circle. I have included two additional charming examples of latticework in merely skeletal form. In one of them the primary and secondary circles are situated on different centers of rotational symmetry; in the other they are concentric (Figure 23.4). Both latticeworks can be found in traditional settings.

Latticeworks are closely related to two-dimensional tessellations: patterns produced by laying down multiple copies of a single shape

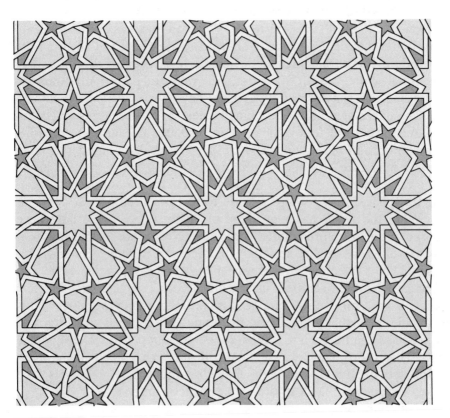

Figure 23.3 Islamic latticework.

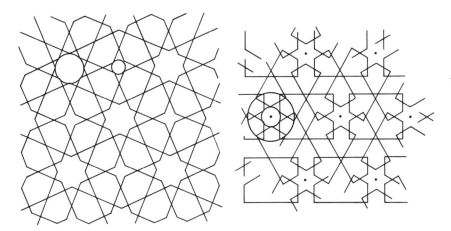

Figure 23.4 Two latticeworks in skeletal form.

without overlap. Each latticework can be produced in the form of a single, finite shape, more specifically a tile. On the tile appears a small part of the overall design. If one has available a great many copies of the tile, one can reproduce the latticework to any extent by laying down enough tiles in the proper way. An examination of any of the latticeworks shown here will reveal a small area in each example that could act as a tile. Here, in any event, lies the prospect for a larger view of any such pattern. Make a tile of sorts on paper and make many copies of it. When the tiles are colored, they lend themselves to a host of decorating ideas.

But what of the original latticework designs? How were they produced and what, for that matter, did they mean? Lisa Golombek has studied the designs for many years, both on site and in her office at the department of Middle East and Islamic studies at the University of Toronto. She thinks some kind of geometric underpinning in the form of grids and circles is the likely method. Undoubtedly individual craftsmen employed variations on the basic technique. As for meaning, Golombek takes issue with the usual explanation that geometric forms were used because of the Islamic prohibition on figurate (human and animal) forms. In her opinion the latticeworks represent a cosmic order that is a hallmark of Islam. For one thing, latticeworks appear in the remains of private residences along with figurative works. In view of the prohibition ignored, the cosmic order obviously appealed to the residents.

It was not altogether correct of me to say that computers have no role to play in the production of latticeworks. Although it may be difficult to program a computer to make the kind of intuitive choices that lead to beautiful patterns, it would be less difficult to write what might be called a computer-aided design program. Such a program would lay out a grid of points according to human choice. The human user might also select the size of the circles, the number of points and so on. When the user of such a program indicates what connections to try, the entire screen would fill with the implication of his or her choice. In short, much of the tedium could be removed. The latticework would emerge, one hopes, from the printer.

Further Reading

Issam El-Said and Ayşe Parman. *Geometric Concepts in Islamic Art.* World of Islam Festival Publishing Company, London, 1976.

ILLUSTRATION CREDITS

Text

Figure 1.4 Courtesy of Brian Silverman, Logo Systems, Montreal

Figure 4.1 Photo © 1989 by Bruce Frisch, Brooklyn, New York

Figures 6.2 and 6.4 Courtesy of Greg Turk

Figure 6.5 Courtesy of Odd Arild Olsen, Oslo, Norway

Figures 10.2–10.4 Courtesy of Mario Markus, Max Planck Institute for Nutrition, Hamburg, Germany

Figures 11.2 and 11.4 Courtesy of Michael Barnsley, Iterated Systems, Inc., Norcross, Georgia

Figure 19.5 Courtesy of Steffen Schindler and Ralf D. Tscheuschner, Institute for Theoretical Physics, University of Hamburg, Germany

Figure 22.1 Courtesy of Clifford A. Pickover, T. J. Watson IBM Research Center, Yorktown Heights, New York

Color insert

Color Plate 1 Copyright © 1993 by O. Christian Irgens, St. Albans, New York; courtesy of The Computer Museum, Boston, Massachusetts

Color Plate 2 Top copyright © 1989, bottom copyright © 1991 by Bruce Frisch, Brooklyn, New York

Color Plate 3 Courtesy of Greg Turk

Color Plate 4 Courtesy of Clifford A. Pickover, T. J. Watson IBM Research Center, Yorktown Heights, New York

INDEX